SUPER CONNECTOR MANIFESTO

Gunil Chung

Paperback ISBN: 978-1-960346-55-1

Published by

\\\ AUTHORSUNITE

*I dedicate this book to my three daughters
for whom I strive to make this world more equitable, habitable,
and loving.
I love you, and I do this for you.*

TABLE OF CONTENTS

INTRODUCTION

"Alone, we can do so little; together, we can do so much."
~ Helen Keller ~

The Leather Apron Club

In Philadelphia, there was once a club known as the *Leather Apron Club*. Founded by an enterprising local newspaper publisher, the first twelve members of this club included a shoemaker, a carpenter, a bartender, and a glassmaker—all tradesmen who wore leather aprons for work, hence the name of the club.

The group met regularly on Friday evenings at a bar and then eventually at a member's house to discuss the latest topics of the day, including developments around town, politics, new scientific discoveries, and even matters of philosophy and morals.

Keep in mind it was more than just an idle social club. Their conversations led to real changes, including the creation of a local fire department and a volunteer group of night watchmen to help reduce crime in the neighborhood. They even founded a hospital!

This club was started in 1727 by none other than Benjamin Franklin. Franklin brought together "ingenious men," the brightest and most industrious people he knew, to create "a club of mutual improvement." He ran it with certain rules in place to ensure there was active participation and healthy debate among the members, "to be conducted in the sincere spirit of inquiry after truth, without fondness for dispute or desire of victory."[1] The club lasted for more than thirty years, and it became so popular that additional chapters were created to accommodate new members.

The Leather Apron Club eventually became the American Philosophical Society, the oldest learned society in the United States, with the mission to "promote useful knowledge." Their website states, "The American Philosophical Society's current activities reflect the founder's spirit of inquiry, provide a forum for the free exchange of ideas, and convey our conviction that intellectual inquiry and critical thought are inherently in the best interest of the public."[2]

Benjamin Franklin is one of the most respected and beloved founding fathers of the United States. The stories of his life are well known, including his work as a successful and irreverent publisher in Philadelphia; his scientific curiosity, which led to the discovery that lightning is actually electricity; his historic mission as the first US Ambassador to a foreign country (France) during a time of great turmoil, the American Revolutionary War; and ultimately his contributions to the founding of the United States after that war.

What is not as well known is the fact that Benjamin Franklin was what you might call a *Super Connector*. He developed and nurtured thousands of relationships across many fields and communities, and these relationships were *essential* to his work. According to the Benjamin Franklin Historical Society:

> "Benjamin Franklin's genius is centered on the use of his network of business and social connections. He leveraged this network to the benefit of his variety of interests from science and politics to business and journalism."[3]

Caroline Winterer, the Anthony P. Meier Family Professor in the Humanities at Stanford University, adds: "What made him especially stand out is the size of his social network and his endless curiosity… Franklin knew he would be nothing without the people around him."[4]

Are You a Super Connector?

So, what exactly is a Super Connector? And if Franklin was one, are there others like him today? Who are they, what do they do, and how do they do it? Can I become a Super Connector myself?

What you are about to read here are the insights distilled from hundreds of conversations I've had with different kinds of Super Connectors, and even several whom I would call "Super Connectors of Super Connectors." Based on these conversations, I've found there are eleven different ways of being a Super Connector, which I describe in this book as *archetypes*. Each archetype has its unique way of connecting with people and helping the communities around them. At the same time, they all share a number of core characteristics that make them excellent at what they do, which make them Super Connectors.

I wrote this book because I believe Super Connectors are exactly what the world needs right now.

We are now living through another time of great turmoil, maybe the greatest ever, with the potential to alter the lives of every living thing on earth. The COVID-19 pandemic took the lives of more than 6.5 million people worldwide and has fundamentally changed the lives of everyone else, with the prospect of more pandemics to come in the future.

Now, as we emerge from several years of the plague, we face other daunting challenges around the world. Plastics and other pollutants plague our oceans, foods, and even our bodies. Rapid climate change is wreaking havoc, with rivers and lakes running dry and catastrophic fires burning millions of acres of land each year, while enough glaciers melt in a single day to submerge entire cities, and millions of people are displaced by floods. In the meantime, wars rage on, killing and injuring untold numbers of people.

Closer to home, we are numb to the news of the senseless mass shootings that claim the lives of thousands of children, teachers, the elderly, and other innocents. We are resigned to other atrocities, big and small, such as hate crimes, police brutality, and more. To top it all off, we are inured to the news of our elected officials being so divided politically that it's almost impossible to do anything constructive to address these problems.

Individually, each of these challenges is daunting; but in aggregate, they seem enormous, even impossible, to address and solve.

But here's the thing. These are not technology problems that require technology solutions. Technology can help, but that's not enough. For example, we have the know-how to develop vaccines against viruses, and we can mass-produce masks to help, but what good are these solutions when we cannot even agree on whether or not we should use them?

These are not even policy problems that require new laws, though again, the right policies can help. How can we enact new legislation to address these challenges if we remain so divided that we cannot even come together as a nation, let alone the world?

Instead, these are *social* problems rooted in our inability to come together across differences, find common ground, develop mutually beneficial solutions, and take collective action. Put another way, these are *communal* problems rooted in our inability to connect with others as brothers and sisters, create community with a shared purpose, advocate for one another, and contribute to the greater good.

We cannot solve these problems alone. There is no amount of water I can shut off in my house to solve the drought problem in California. There is no amount of recycling I can do by myself to get rid of all the plastics in the ocean. It is literally impossible for us *individually* to solve these challenges. We must act together.

This is where Super Connectors come in.

By definition, Super Connectors are people who are exceptional at building, maintaining, and deepening trusted, meaningful relationships across social boundaries and at scale. They are relationship-focused people who operate with the currency of trust. They are community organizers who bring people together across differences. They are ambassadors who build bridges across different communities. They are catalysts who rally communities toward collective action. They are culture keepers who help to maintain the values that are dear to us, values that sustain the communities around us.

In short, Super Connectors are people who are extraordinarily good at bringing other people together for mutual benefit. They can help us to *collectively* address the major challenges we all face. If we are to have a chance at making it through this time of great turmoil, then we need these Super Connectors to help bring the world together.

That is why this book is titled *Super Connector Manifesto*. This is a *manifesto*, a call for Super Connectors to recognize themselves, rise up, and do what they do best: help us unite and make it through these challenges.

Conversations with Super Connectors

Who am I to write about Super Connectors? For the better part of two decades, I have worked as a connector and a community builder. First, at an international think tank for senior technology executives at Fortune 500 companies, I built and ran executive communities where members met to discuss important and sensitive topics in a trusted environment. Then, at a Fortune 500 technology company, I leveraged my relationships to enable the first $100 million deal in the history of the firm and many other large transactions after that.

At another Silicon Valley technology startup, I leveraged my connector skills to help the company grow from $100 million in annual revenue to more than $1 billion in annual revenue. I've run an online community where tens of thousands of entrepreneurs come together to share best practices and help one another. I've run a nonprofit that hosted executive roundtables, dinners, and events for business leaders in New York City. All along the way, I've made an untold number of connections for people. So, I know a thing or two about being a connector.

This book, however, is not about me. Instead, this book is about the hundreds of other Super Connectors I've met and interviewed. While I might be good at what I do, I knew there were others who were *exceptional* at it. I was curious about what they do and how they do it. What jobs do they have, and how did they get there? What makes them excellent, and what do they all have in common? If I could distill their best practices, what would I find, and how could I learn from them to become better myself? Even more importantly, how could I share what I learn with others who realize they are also Super Connectors so they can have even greater positive impacts on the world?

To help answer those questions, this book is organized into the following chapters:

Chapter 1: What Makes Super Connectors Super. In this chapter, I define what I mean by *Super Connector* and describe the core common traits that make them *super*.

Chapter 2: Matchmaker. In this chapter, I introduce the first and foundational archetype, the Matchmaker. Matchmakers make connections that literally change people's lives. They have a deep curiosity about people and have an instinctive desire and ability to help others by connecting them with each other.

Chapter 3: Superhost. A Superhost is someone who excels at bringing people together into gatherings where there is a sense of "home, hearth, and hygge." They build on the power of the Matchmaker to host events where people feel at home and can connect genuinely with one another.

Chapter 4: Community Builder. A Community Builder builds on the power of the Superhost to create a community that lasts over time beyond just one event. A community has an identity of its own, a unifying purpose, a guiding set of values, and creates many opportunities for its members to get together and connect over time.

Chapter 5: Catalyst. The Catalyst excels at bringing people together for a mission. They are change agents and agitators, compelled toward a goal, and are especially good at harnessing the power of a community to achieve that goal.

Chapter 6: Seer. Seers see through conversations. They have an amazing capacity for connecting the dots across many conversations with people in different fields, deriving new insights from those conversations, and then sharing that back to the community.

Chapter 7: Innovator. Innovators are excellent at bringing other people together to invent new things. They bust the myth of the lone genius who has a "Eureka" moment and instead demonstrate how a Super Connector can bring together a group of people with a diverse set of skills to co-invent something new for the world.

Chapter 8: Advocate. Advocates are great at identifying people within a community who have the experiences, skills, and perspectives the community needs and then advocating for those people. The advocate connects them with others in the community in such a way that benefits everyone involved.

Chapter 9: Ambassador. Ambassadors excel at bringing two or more communities together toward a shared goal with their mutual interests in mind. In doing so, they amplify the impact of the communities involved and serve the needs of a broader set of people.

Chapter 10: Explorer. Explorers excel at finding helpful people, resources, and ideas from faraway communities and bringing them back to their home communities. They explore not just places but communities of people.

Chapter 11: Elder. The Elder is a member of the community whom others look up to because of their many contributions to the community. Their special contribution is that they are the culture keepers of the community, and thus help maintain the integrity of the community.

Chapter 12: The Sage. The Sage is the Super Connector who can inhabit multiple Super Connector archetypes with mastery and ease. While most Super Connectors naturally inhabit more than one archetype, the Sage is excellent at multiple archetypes and can switch from one to the next with ease. They are often excellent as mentors and teachers for the next generation of Super Connectors.

Chapter 13: Energy Management. Being a Super Connector requires sustained effort over time. This chapter offers practical advice on how Super Connectors manage their energy to be successful and effective over time.

Chapter 14: Technology Enablers. In this chapter, we'll explore how Super Connectors use technology to amplify and scale their efforts, from simple notecards and spreadsheets to sophisticated relationship management systems.

Chapter 15: Riding the Super Connector Highway. What happens when you have a Super Connector of Super Connectors? In this chapter, I'll show examples of such communities of Super Connectors and what they are doing to help tackle some of the most difficult and complex challenges we all face.

Chapter 16: Conclusion – The Manifesto. I conclude with a call to arms for Super Connectors to rise, take up the challenge, and help bring people and communities together. The world is divided, and we can only address the world's challenges together.

Who Is This Book For?

If you identify as a Super Connector or if others have called you one, then I hope you recognize yourself in one or more archetypes described in these pages and that these stories and descriptions help inform who you are. Furthermore, I hope this book inspires you to *lean into* your gifts and do more to help bring the world together to tackle the world's challenges. The time is now, and without you, the task ahead is much more difficult.

If you identify as a connector but are not yet sure if you would describe yourself as being Super, this book is also for you. I have met many people who have the core traits and tendencies of a Super Connector but, for various reasons, have not fully tapped into their talents. I hope you see aspects of yourself in these pages and that the examples herein provide useful guidance for how to develop your skills, connect with others, and manifest yourself as a Super Connector.

Lastly, even if you don't identify as a connector or a Super Connector, I hope this book helps you by showing you who they are. They are your colleagues, family members, friends, and neighbors. They do what they do because it's in their nature, and they're great at it, but they need your help! You might be *just* the person an Innovator is looking for with the right skills needed for an important project or the expert an Explorer is looking for to help make a perilous journey possible. Or maybe you manage a Super Connector in your organization and are in a position to offer opportunities to fully leverage their powers. Or you might be the neighbor who brings the perfect dish to a potluck dinner organized by a Superhost. In the end, Super Connectors cannot do this on their own. After all, they bring people together, and you are likely one of those people!

Introduction Notes

1. For more information on Franklin's Leather Apron Club, see https://en.wikipedia.org/wiki/Junto_(club).
2. See About the APS: https://www.amphilsoc.org/about.
3. See http://www.benjamin-franklin-history.org/benjamin-franklin.
4. See https://news.stanford.edu/press-releases/2018/11/12/benjamin-franklin-social-genius-18th-century.

CHAPTER 1:
WHAT MAKES SUPER
CONNECTORS SUPER?

"Trust is the glue of life. It's the most essential ingredient in effective communication.
It's the foundational principle that holds all relationships."
~ Stephen Covey ~

What do a Russian immigrant matchmaker, an executive coach from Morocco living in Seattle, the daughter of a travel agent, a self-described Kansas farmboy, a sought-after expert in the healthcare industry, the co-founder of the largest hate group in America, a refugee from Nepal, the first man to walk both the North and South poles and a global philanthropist all have in common?

They are all examples of the Super Connectors you'll read about in this book. As random and diverse as this group of people may seem to be, they and others like them all share certain core traits that make them "Super" at what they do. In this chapter, I define what it means to be a Super Connector and describe the core traits they all share.

Let's start with the definition. Super Connectors are people who are exceptional at building, maintaining, and deepening trusted, meaningful relationships across social boundaries and at scale. Fundamentally, they make connections for other people, connections that change people's lives.

Let's delve into the definition to see how Super Connectors do what they do.

They Build Relationships Based on Trust

We all get what it means to build, maintain, and deepen relationships. We are social creatures, and even the most introverted among us do this. But Super Connectors do so with *trust* as the foundation of their relationships. Whether consciously or intuitively, Super Connectors know how to earn and keep trust, how to build and expand on that trust with every connection they make (thus expanding their "circles of trust"), and how to build communities with trust at the center.

To do that, they have to be trust*worthy*, and there are four elements to being trustworthy: character, competence, consistency, and community.

Character: Who are you as a person, and do you care about me and my well-being, or are you just after your own personal gain? If your intentions are suspect, people will figure that out sooner or later, and you won't have their trust. It's that simple.

Competence: If your intentions are good and helpful toward others, but you just don't have the ability to do the work, that doesn't build trust either. Would you trust a first-year medical student to perform surgery on you? Competence in your craft instills trust. Competence is also contextual. Would you trust a world-class surgeon to repair your car?

Consistency: Do you demonstrate your character and competence consistently over time? Trust is earned over time by repeatedly doing what you said you would do. Michael Keithley, the CIO at the United Talent Agency and a Super Connector, shared how he focuses on "shortening the *say-do gap*." In other words, what is the gap between what you say and what you do, and how do you get that gap to be as close to zero as possible? And then do that consistently, time after time, with every interaction.

Community: The community that you're a part of can bestow a level of trust to you. So even before someone gets to know you, the community that you're associated with and the people you know can confer a certain level of trust (or lack thereof) to you. How often do people use "backchannels" to vet a candidate for an important role? The main difference between the above three factors and this one is that the others are *intrinsic* to you while this is *extrinsic*. The point here isn't that you should seek to join a high-trust community to increase your trust; rather that trust does not happen in a vacuum. It's relational and communal, and this is especially relevant for Super Connectors.

Being trustworthy does not automatically make you a Super Connector. But without being trustworthy, you cannot be a Super Connector. There is no way around building deep relationships over a long period of time without trust.

They Form Meaningful Relationships

Super Connectors are adept at forming meaningful, personal relationships that go beyond the title, beyond the transaction, to really connect with others as human beings. They have the courage to be authentic and vulnerable with others, regardless of their backgrounds and positions.

Lt. Colonel Jen "JJ" Snow (retired), and an amazing Super Connector herself, says it this way: "Many people operate transactionally: 'You give me this, and I'll give you that.' Relationships become exponentially more meaningful and powerful when it's trust-based and focused on mutual value."

They Form Relationships
Across Social Boundaries

There are many social boundaries around us: racial, political, religious, socioeconomic, organizational, cultural, and so on. These social boundaries often divide and separate us from one another. For example, think about how people "unfriend" one another on social media over differences big and small; or how religious and political affiliations divide family members. These social boundaries can be very difficult to cross.

Super Connectors are often able to operate past such perceived differences and connect with other people as humans—as brothers, sisters, aunts, and uncles. I call that "seeing brother, not other." By doing so, they are able to bring people together and make meaningful connections across these social boundaries.

They Nurture Relationships at Scale Over Time

They do all this at scale, with not just hundreds but thousands, and sometimes even tens of thousands of people.

Robin Dunbar, a British anthropologist, theorized in 1993 that humans could have no more than about 150 meaningful relationships at any one time. He argued we simply do not have the mental capacity for more than that, and he cited biological, historical, and sociological evidence to show this is a real phenomenon. If Dunbar is correct, how can Super Connectors exist, and how do they manage to have tens of thousands of meaningful relationships over time?

Super Connectors, like everyone else, are limited to just twenty-four hours a day and can actively engage with only a finite number of people at any one time, but—and this is key—they have found ways to keep hundreds or even thousands of relationships active and meaningful over long stretches of time. They do this by building high levels of trust and social capital with others, by leveraging communities to engage with other people at scale, and by being proactive and thoughtful about their relationships. Their ability to scale deep relationships over time is part of what makes them *Super*, and we'll explore this aspect in more detail in chapters 13 and 14.

They Make Connections *for Other People*

Being a Super Connector is not about having millions of followers or thousands of online connections. You might call that being "Super-Connected" Of course, Super Connectors are well-connected with thousands of relationships, but one of the key distinctions of Super Connectors is that they make connections *for other people*. That's what makes them Super *Connectors*.

These connections often change the lives of the people being connected. Imagine what happens when a Matchmaker brings two people together who wind up falling in love, or when an Innovator brings a diverse group of people together to invent something new, or when an Ambassador brings two communities together to help heal deep communal wounds. Their lives are forever changed.

This is what Super Connectors *do*. They build, maintain, and deepen trusted, meaningful relationships across social boundaries and at scale. Fundamentally, they make connections for other people, connections that change people's lives.

Super Connectors, regardless of their archetype, all share the following core traits that enable them to do what they do. In other words, these are the core traits of all Super Connectors.

1. **They are Trustworthy:** They work hard to earn and keep the trust of others.
2. **They are Curious:** They are genuinely curious about people and the world around them.
3. **They are Emotionally Intelligent:** They have high EQ (emotional intelligence), enabling them to understand and connect with people quickly and authentically.
4. **They are Givers, not Takers:** They are not transactional, and they do not keep score. Instead, they are driven by a deep desire to help others. [Refer to Adam Grant's book, *Give and Take*]
5. **They have Community Intelligence:** They have an innate awareness and appreciation for communities, including how to create, develop, and work with them.
6. **They are Purpose-Driven:** They are often driven by a larger purpose or goal that involves helping other people in some way.

Angela Yochem, the Global Chief Information Officer at Krispy Kreme and before that, the Chief Transformation and Digital Officer at Novant Health, sums it up beautifully here and highlights the above core traits of Super Connectors:

"Super connectors are driven to understand ever-expanding context, and as a result (without any effort applied other than exercising our curiosity), we are consistently reaching out, getting involved in broad efforts for good, meeting interesting people doing great work, building communities, expanding communities, finding win/win/wins, and so on. Super connectors have an outrageously large network not only because the work that they do attracts others but because they actively strive to learn about and engage in great work happening elsewhere, finding ways to ensure that good work is impactful and elevated. The winning of hearts and minds is natural because super connectors are interested in (curious about) what is in others' hearts and minds. These types of people tend to be inspirational leaders and lifelong learners. They never stop being intensely curious."

Super Connectors Connect People

Ultimately, this is the defining aspect of Super Connectors: They make connections for other people, connections that change people's lives. Their natural curiosity, high EQ, and generous nature help draw people around them. Their trustworthiness and intelligence about communities help them to deepen and scale their relationships over time. Their purpose drives them to expand their circles of trust, making connections for other people in pursuit of their goals. All the archetypes described in this book fundamentally connect people, though they do so differently, according to their type. You may already have various questions about Super Connectors. Feel free to read Appendix A: Frequently Asked Questions.

This leads us to the next chapter and the first archetype: the Matchmaker. The Matchmaker is the most fundamental archetype for all Super Connectors and a great lens for understanding how Super Connectors connect people.

CHAPTER 2:
THE MATCHMAKER

"My favorite hobby is matchmaking. It's a lot easier to do it in movies than in real life because in real life, people don't do what I tell them to do."
~ Susanne Bier ~
(Golden Globe, Emmy, and Academy Award winning writer and director)

The social isolation of the COVID-19 pandemic resulted in a significant rise in the use of dating apps as singles looked online to connect with each other. According to *Vox*, "all the activities related to online dating ratcheted up during the pandemic,"[1] with *Fortune Magazine* noting that one of the popular dating apps "saw a 700% increase in dates" between March and May of 2020 alone.[2]

In a similar way, professional matchmakers saw their businesses boom during the pandemic. This was partially sparked by the awareness about matchmakers from shows like *Millionaire Matchmaker* but was fueled by the sheer effort and fatigue that can come from using dating apps. The founder of one matchmaking service estimates that "the average online dater spends 12 hours a week online" looking for a match, which is "like having a part-time job."[3] Essentially, many singles would like to outsource the time-consuming effort of vetting hundreds of profiles and just go straight to meeting a few high-quality candidates.

If quality is what we're after, then what distinguishes a great matchmaker from a less successful one? What do the best matchmakers do to find the perfect match for their clients? The answers to these questions shed light on the "Matchmaker" archetype and highlight the core traits all Super Connectors share.

Anna Morgenstern

To help us with these questions, let me introduce Anna Morgenstern. Anna is one of the best, most sought-after matchmakers and dating coaches in New York City. She saw her business double during the pandemic and worked diligently to help her clients connect with new romantic partners.

That said, being a professional matchmaker is not something she had ever thought about while growing up. She was born into a family of Russian-Jewish immigrants living in Monterey, California, and as with many other children of immigrants, she struggled to fit in. At home, she felt pressure from her parents to come home right after school, study hard, and get good grades. While at school, she wanted to make friends, join after-school activities, go to parties, and maybe even date. It didn't help that she was painfully shy, and her sense of isolation deepened when her only sibling (her older sister) went off to college, leaving her to fend for herself at home and at school.

So how did she go from being a shy, lonely child of immigrants who did not date to being a top professional matchmaker and relationship coach in New York City, with hundreds of grateful clients all around the world? Hint: The journey to being a matchmaker began after her older sister left for college.

Before we tell the rest of her story, however, let's take a look at the Matchmaker archetype.

The Matchmaker

The first Super Connector archetype is the Matchmaker. By that, I don't mean they are all romantic matchmakers who connect you with potential partners. What I mean instead is that matching and connecting people with each other is a fundamental activity of all Super Connectors. As we talked about in the previous chapter, Super

Connectors make connections that can literally change people's lives, as Anna does when she connects her clients with their future life partners.

So, it follows that there are different examples of the Matchmaker archetype. Some illustrative examples include dating matchmakers (like Anna) who connect people with each other for love, executive recruiters who connect job seekers with those who are hiring, and real estate agents who connect home buyers with home sellers.

While these Matchmakers have turned their penchant for connecting people into a career, there are many others who don't do it for work or money. They just do it. If you're lucky, you may even know some people like this. They are often found saying things like, "Oh, you're going to Austin? Let me connect you to my friend." Most people do this to some degree, of course, but for Matchmakers, it's almost a compulsion. They can't help but think this way and derive great satisfaction from helping people by connecting them to each other. And they're great at it!

If this description resonates with you, congratulations, you may be a Matchmaker!

Now let's see how the core traits of all Super Connectors manifest with the Matchmaker archetype.

Trustworthy: Would you take a call or an introduction from someone whom you did not trust? Angela Yochem said this to me one time when I was making an introduction for her, and it was brilliant. She said simply, "I trust you to make meaningful connections for me." First, she expressed her trust in me, which I deeply appreciated. Second, she reminded me of my responsibility to only make introductions that are meaningful and of mutual value to her and the other person. Super Connectors become trusted by others to make connections that are valuable for everyone involved.

Curious: Matchmakers are deeply curious about other people. This is what enables them to get to know these people well enough to make life-changing connections. They get to know people in meaningful ways beyond the surface, such as what makes them unique and special, their goals and aspirations, their hobbies, who their loved ones are, and so on.

Emotionally Intelligent: It goes without saying that Matchmakers have high EQ. Making matches for people is not just an intellectual exercise with a checklist of facts. If it were, dating apps would be much more successful! There is a deep emotional component that helps the Matchmaker to see if there will be "chemistry" between them.

Givers not Takers: It's true that there are Matchmakers who have turned their knack for making great connections into a career. But for many Matchmakers, this comes from an almost instinctive desire to help others through connections, without wanting anything back in return. They don't keep score. Tony Leng, one of the best executive recruiters in the US, often makes very thoughtful professional introductions for the people he knows, and most of the time, there is nothing "in it" for him except knowing he was able to help his clients and friends.

Community Intelligence: In the purest sense, this trait is the least evident with Matchmakers, as they focus more on making one-to-one connections rather than building community. Yet they often participate in and leverage communities to make new connections and deepen existing ones. For example, Anna Morgenstern often brings her clients to social events (communities) to see how they are "in real life," and connects them to potential matches there.

Speaking of Anna, let's go back to her story to see how she became a world-class matchmaker.

Her journey to eventually being a professional matchmaker began when she was ten years old after her older sister left for college. Her parents had been highly educated and skilled professionals in Russia—her father was a geologist, and her mother was an accountant—but in the US, their degrees and experiences did not matter much. They ended up taking menial jobs and working "crazy long hours" to make a living in their newly adopted country.

As a result, Anna did not see much of her parents. She and her older sister would come home from school on their own, make their own meals, do their homework, and generally look after themselves until their parents returned home late in the evening, tired from the day's toil.

After her older sister went off to college, Anna's sense of isolation and loneliness was profound. This sense persisted for years and turned into a deep desire for the young Anna to connect with her peers, make friends, and belong.

Fortunately for Anna, she found out she inherited her parents' outgoing nature and gift for connecting with people. Her father had been working as a janitor in the office building of a geology company. He struck up a friendship with the staff, and when they found out he was a trained geologist, they offered him a job. Her mother, meanwhile, had been working as a maid at a hotel, but she loved having fresh flowers at home, so she developed a friendship with the owner of her favorite flower shop. She ended up getting a job doing accounting at the shop, which then led to an accounting position at the local university. Anna overcame her initial shyness and discovered she could be very outgoing, just like her parents.

Furthermore, as she became a young adult, she discovered she was like her mother in another important way: She found herself thinking about her friends and matching them up with each other. She explained, "My Mother's interest in other people's love lives definitely transferred over to me, and even before I was a professional matchmaker, I was constantly setting up my friends with each other."

After graduating from college, she moved to New York City to pursue a career in advertising. She made many new friends in the city and continued to set up her friends with each other. In fact, she was so successful as a matchmaker that she started to think about making it her career. One incident in particular convinced her to do it, and this story illustrates the secret to being a great Matchmaker.

> "This was the summer of 2015. One of my best friends really wanted to meet and marry a Jewish man, but wasn't happy with the ones that she had dated so far. One weekend that summer, we were having a birthday party for her. When we ran out of beer, I went downstairs to the bodega to get more. I was in line when I heard a guy with a British accent behind me make fun of a tattoo on my back. I turned around and saw that he was wearing a large Star of David necklace. I grabbed him and told him to go home, change, and come to the party in his best outfit. 'You are about to meet your wife', I told him. He arrived at the party a short while later and met my friend. They have been together ever since, and now they share two beautiful babies. Sometimes matchmaking is a science but more often than not, it's a feeling. I just knew my friend needed to meet this guy."

The not-so-secret secret to her success is that she knew her friend *so well* (this was her best friend, after all) that she just knew, at a glance, this was the man for her. Matchmakers excel at what they do by getting to know you really well and caring enough to make connections for you. They use their curiosity and high EQ to really get to know you. In effect, they become your friend, and because they know you so well, they can make great connections for you, connections that are meaningful and valuable for you. Put another way, they care to get to know you and make the effort to connect you with the right person or people. It takes effort, but it's that simple.

Tony Leng

Now let's consider another example of the Matchmaker archetype. This is the story of Tony Leng, one of the top executive recruiters in the US who focuses on placing technology leaders.

Tony was born and raised in South Africa where he said he led a "privileged early life." He attended the top high school and university in the country, where he excelled in both academics and sports. After graduation, he was thrust into the "deep end of big business" as a young professional across various industries, eventually becoming the CEO of three different companies.

Then in 1999, he made the fateful decision to move to the US. "It became too dangerous to live in South Africa and I didn't feel that my family and I were safe," he explained. They arrived in San Francisco on January 1, 2020, and moved into a three-bedroom, two-bath apartment in the city. In South Africa, they had lived in a large mansion staffed with servants. "My kids barely noticed the difference, but it was hard on my wife," he shared.

It was difficult for Tony, too. He recalled, "I didn't know anyone, any company. I went from being amazingly well-connected as a CEO in South Africa, to not knowing anyone at all. It was massively humbling." He was forty-three at the time, with his wife and four sons to provide for. To make matters worse, he had just accepted a position as an executive recruiter where the job required him to know lots of people!

So how did he do it? How did he go from not knowing anyone to being one of the top executive recruiters in the country? He stated simply, "I had to build everything from the ground up."

Tony's story here is a great illustration of a Super Connector Matchmaker in action. As you read about it, please keep in mind the definition of a Super Connector and its key traits of Trust, Curiosity, EQ, Giver, and Community, as well as the fact that Super Connectors ultimately make connections for other people.

Leveraging Communities

First, he tapped the Young Presidents' Organization (YPO), where he had been a member for many years during his time in South Africa. YPO describes itself on its website as follows: "We are the global leadership community of extraordinary chief executives — more than 30,000 members around the world, coming together to become better leaders and better people." One of their rules is that if another member reaches out to you, you are obliged to respond within a certain amount of time. The call may not lead to anything, and most of the members are careful to not abuse that privilege. But Tony took advantage of that network and reached out to the executives he thought might have work for him.

Unfortunately, most of the CEOs he reached out to did not have work for him, but what Tony did next is telling. He asked these CEOs to connect him to *other leaders* they thought might have work for him. *Those* connections were much more fruitful for him.

This ability to leverage existing communities is a key skill for Super Connectors. Furthermore, research shows there is immense value in your "friends of friends." While your first-degree connections (your friends) may not be able to help you, *their* friends (your second-degree connections) often can. Tony intuitively tapped into this power of communities.

Build Trust with Every Interaction

Second, he made sure to make the most of those opportunities and build trust (and his reputation) with every engagement. "I made a big meal out of a few ingredients," he shared. Simply put, he went the extra mile. For example, he made it a point to meet with his clients in person rather than by phone. He over-prepared and came in with insights and ideas his clients did not anticipate. It helped that he had years of experience as the CEO of large companies in South Africa, and he amplified his experience with effort. He always worked hard to follow through and deliver for his clients. Recall the earlier point that Michael Keithley made about "shortening the say-do gap" and how Trust is a function of character, competence, consistency, and community. One client at a time, Tony built trust, his reputation, his network, and his new life in the US.

Give to Others

Third, he gave generously to his contacts and went out of his way to help them as much as possible. For example, he made himself available to speak at events. He learned as much as he could about the world of technology through his numerous conversations with senior leaders, as well as through his own personal research. Then he offered to speak for free at various events where his potential clients and recruits would attend. This helped the event organizers, the attendees, and his reputation.

Another example is how he built a community of his own. His company website states, "For the past seventeen years, Leng has also facilitated the Fisher CIO Forum, a monthly venue where CDOs, CIOs, and CTOs discuss topics of strategic relevance, learn, network, and seek peer group input on a confidential basis." The participants are potential clients and recruits, and he gave his time and effort generously to curate this network, bring the people together, and add value. He does not charge for this community, but he works hard to continue to bring the group together and add value through insights, friendship, and support.

Connect People

Fourth, he connects people. Of course, as an executive recruiter, that is his job, to connect well-qualified candidates to the executive who is hiring. He uses his years of experience as a CEO and as a recruiter to assess and find the best candidates, and he works with both sides to help ensure a great fit.

He goes above and beyond that, however, to connect the people he knows to each other for mutual benefit. I recently reached out to Tony to ask if he could recommend Artificial Intelligence and Machine Learning (AI/ML) experts to speak on a panel, and he immediately replied with the names of four amazing people. He then followed up with them to make introductions where it was welcome. He does this for his friends and colleagues all the time.

Today, he is one of the best executive recruiters in the country, having earned the trust and friendship of thousands of technology leaders, as well as the CEOs and company board members who are hiring for these technology leaders.

Matchmaker Best Practices

Here are several ways people who identify as the Matchmaker archetype of Super Connector excel at what they do:

1. Quality Over Quantity

The world is full of unsolicited outreaches, discarded business cards, and digital connections on professional networking sites where you don't remember the person or even how you met them. If you want to make a connection for someone, make it count! Focus on the *quality* and *impact* of each introduction, rather than the quantity of connections.

2. Be Clear About the Value for Both Sides

Often, someone (A) will ask you for an introduction to someone else (B) because the former wants something from the latter. Before you make that connection, be clear on the value to the latter (B), and make sure the value is clear, genuine, and compelling. If not, then consider politely declining person A. This will protect the trust you have with person B, but will also increase the trust with person A, who will see how you treat relationships (including with person A) with respect.

3. When Making an Introduction, Make it a Love Letter

How often do you get an email or note saying "you two should meet," without a clear explanation for who that other person is, who they mean to the person making the introduction, and the purpose of the connection. Take the time to explain who each person is, not just in terms of their professional background, but what you find so special about them in this context, and who they are to you. Let the love (or at least esteem) you have for both people come through in your note!

4. Look for the Win/Win/Win

Is there a higher-level value in the introduction than what the two parties will get? Are you strengthening the community around you? Are you advancing a cause they both (and you) care about? This is partially how you contribute to the greater good, one amazing, life-changing introduction at a time.

Next, let's consider the second Super Connector archetype, a close cousin of the Matchmaker: the Superhost. Just like the Matchmaker, you probably know someone in your life who is a Superhost. I'll start this next chapter with an illustrative story.

Chapter 2 Notes

1. See https://www.vox.com/recode/22348298/tinder-data-video-online-dating-pandemic.
2. See https://fortune.com/2021/02/12/covid-pandemic-online-dating-apps-usage-tinder-okcupid-bumble-meet-group.
3. See https://www.bostonglobe.com/lifestyle/2019/04/22/how-hire-matchmaker/lHg1giWcT86YwKzO9Y8EfM/story.html.

CHAPTER 3:
THE SUPERHOST

"Hygge: a quality of coziness and comfortable conviviality that engenders a feeling of contentment or well-being (regarded as a defining characteristic of Danish culture)."
~ The Oxford English Dictionary ~

Nora Paxton

Nora Paxton is a successful executive coach based in Seattle, Washington. As with other Super Connectors, she knows lots of people, with thousands of clients around the world, more than 17,000 followers on LinkedIn, and friends wherever she goes. There was a time, however, when she didn't know anyone and, like Tony Leng, had to start from scratch. What she did to make new friends is a great illustration of the next archetype, the Superhost.

Nora's story begins in Casablanca, Morocco, where she was born as the first of three daughters to her parents. Her father was an ex-athlete turned diplomat, and her mother was an exuberant extrovert who loved to cook dinner feasts for their family and friends. Because of her father's work as a diplomat, her childhood memories are of moving from place to place all the time, including France, England, Italy, and Spain. When asked, she struggles to say where she's from because they didn't stay in one place long enough to really call any of them home. Home was wherever they were, with the aroma of her mother's cooking filling the house and the sounds of different languages spoken merging into a happy din.

As a self-described "extra-extrovert," Nora thrived in this environment. Even as a young three-year-old girl, she easily remembered details about her parents' dinner guests, including their jobs, the names of their family members, and other distinguishing details. She loved meeting new people all the time and was never shy about striking up a conversation with strangers. She commented, "I've always gone up to people without having to know them!" Her curiosity and love for people carried over into her school years where she connected easily with her teachers and friends.

Professionally, she flourished in her job in software sales, where she got to travel all over Europe, as she did when she was growing up, meeting new people and making new friends. It helped that she was passionate about her work and the product she was selling, and she was thus able to "close all my deals." She reflected that the key to her success was how she genuinely cared about her clients. She could quickly understand their pain points and easily match the value of the product to what her clients needed.

It was after she married and moved to Seattle—where her husband had his job—when she hit a wall. She knew absolutely no one in Seattle. "I was in Seattle, no one knew me, and I had to start from zero," she recalled.

At this point, you might see a similar pattern as with the story of Tony Leng: two otherwise happy and successful people who moved to another country (the US) where they didn't know anyone. This dislocation is not universal for all Super Connectors, but when it does happen, they instinctively turn to their powers to make new friends and build a new community around them. In Tony's case, he reached out to the Young Presidents' Organization to make new connections for work. Nora took a different approach, one that highlights the powers of the Superhost. Simply put, she set out to make new friends by hosting dinner parties, just like her mother used to do.

The Superhost

The term "Superhost" was first coined in 2009 by Airbnb, the online marketplace where you can rent other people's homes on a short-term basis, "to recognize the early hosts who helped set a high standard for hosting on Airbnb."[1] These were the best hosts who consistently went above and beyond to deliver an excellent experience for their guests. It's a fitting word from a company whose motto is *Belong Anywhere*.

In the context of this book, Superhosts are Super Connectors who host gatherings where many people can come together to meet and connect with one another in a convivial setting. These gatherings do not have to be dinner parties; they can be lunches, game nights, birthday parties, or even a dip in an icy lake (as we'll see later). Regardless of the venue, as they bring people together, Superhosts create a sense of *home, hearth, and hygge* that enables the guests to connect with one another in a fun and genuine way.

First, they make their guests feel welcome and at *home*, that they belong at the gathering. Second, they create some kind of a *hearth*, be it a dinner table, a game, or a shared activity, around which the guests can congregate. And third, by doing so, they create a sense of *hygge*, or well-being, for everyone. Let's go back to Nora to see how she does this.

Home

First, Superhosts make their guests feel welcome and at home. Nora invited everyone she knew, including her neighbors, work colleagues, acquaintances from church, book club friends, and anyone else she met. When they showed up at her dinner parties, she went out of her way, happily and genuinely, to make them feel welcome and at home. For example, she makes it a point to greet everyone at the door herself. She admits she's a hugger, and she welcomes everyone to her house with a big warm hug.

It doesn't have to always be at someone's house to make people feel at *home*. Nora certainly opens up her house to her guests, but my good friend Rebecca Friese, a best-selling author and expert on workplace culture, has for years hosted a women's lunch event called *12 at 12* at various local restaurants.

Another example is Yousuf Khan, a partner at the venture capital firm, Ridge Ventures, in Silicon Valley, California. For many years, when he was working as the chief information officer at a number of technology startup companies in Silicon Valley, he made it a point to bring together other chief information officers he liked and admired into regular social gatherings for drinks and dinner at various local restaurants in the Bay Area. These gatherings became as much a part of his signature style as the sweater vests he loves to wear.

The key is how Superhosts make their guests feel welcome and at home, regardless of the venue.

Hearth

Superhosts create a *hearth* around which people can gather and enjoy each other's company. The hearth could literally be a fireplace, but more often than not, it's a warm dinner table, a fun evening of charades, a watch party for a big game, a festive birthday party, and so forth. The hearth is something around which the attendees can congregate and meet.

Nora loves to cook, as her mother did, and makes most of the dishes herself. She usually makes Moroccan and French dishes. For Moroccan, she loves to make chicken tagine with preserved lemons and olives, or lamb with dried prunes and apricots. "My guests always enjoyed my Moroccan dishes as they are unique and flavorful and they combine many spices such as Cumin, Coriander, and Ginger." For French, she favors baking brioches or quiches. "My favorite French dishes are my quiches as they are quick and easy to make and can incorporate all sorts of ingredients."

She doesn't just offer up a meal, but creates an experience for her guests. She explained, "I enjoy cooking alone because I enjoy doing it fast. I learned that from my mother! And then I spend time around the kitchen island with my guests to explain how I made my dishes. I usually explain the origin of the dish then take my guest through its preparation and then maybe show how locals eat it."

She goes beyond the meal to provide opportunities for the guests to meet. For example, she often hosts card games after dinner where there are fun questions on the cards that allow people to get to know each other. It's not just about creating an entertaining experience for her guests, but rather fostering ways for her guests to meet and become better friends. Sometimes she will pointedly invite people who "need a little cheering up," and who doesn't need that from time to time?

A hearth is something around which the participants can gather, have a shared experience, and get to know each other. Why do you need a hearth? Imagine if Nora invited her guests to her home but left everyone to fend for themselves. It wouldn't work, would it? Not only that, it's hard to imagine Nora doing such a thing. As a Superhost, she makes the effort to create a hearth around which people can gather and become better acquainted with each other.

Hygge

Ultimately, it's about having everyone experience a sense of *hygge* together. According to the Oxford English dictionary, *hygge* is a Danish word meaning "a quality of coziness and comfortable conviviality that engenders a feeling of contentment or well-being." It's the feeling of cozy contentment that comes from sitting next to a fireplace with a few good friends on a cold evening, wrapped in a warm blanket, sipping hot chocolate. It's the feeling you get when you're gathered with your family over a holiday, sharing food and stories with one another. It's the feeling young Nora had when her mother would host dinner parties for their friends and everyone would speak in multiple languages. And it's the feeling she engenders for her guests now at her home in Seattle.

The key is in the *togetherness* with others, gathered around the *hearth*, and feeling welcome and at *home* there. Nora, and other Superhosts like her, intuitively know how to create this sense of *hygge*.

How are Matchmakers and Superhosts Different?

Simply put, the Matchmaker connects one person with another, while the Superhost creates a gathering where people can connect with each other. One approach is not inherently better than the other; it's just a different way that Super Connectors manifest themselves. The Matchmaker emphasizes the connection itself and makes introductions that can literally change people's lives. The Superhost creates an *environment* within which people can connect with each other in a meaningful way.

As another illustrative example, let's consider the story of another Nora: Nora Ephron, the American journalist, writer, and filmmaker, whose dinner parties were legendary. Lynda Obst, the American producer for movies like *Flashdance*, *Contact*, and *Interstellar*, recalled: "Nora Ephron was one of my best friends and mentors. She gave the greatest dinner parties in the world!"[2]

There were a few things that Nora Ephron did consistently to create these amazing dinner parties. For one, she always insisted on having a large round dining table, so everyone could participate in the conversation, instead of being left out at the end of a long rectangular table. She had seating charts so it would not be awkward for people to think about where to sit, and so she could strategically place people she wanted to connect next to each other. She also had a "Rule of Four," which was basically that in addition to meats, carbs, and vegetables, there should be a fourth, surprising element to the dinner course. Finally, she would entertain her guests with a game of charades. You can see an example of this in the movie *When Harry Met Sally*, for which Nora wrote the screenplay.[3]

Superhosts create a gathering where people can connect with each other. For example, Lynda Obst met a woman named Ann Druyan at a dinner party Nora Ephron hosted in 1974. Ann is an Emmy and Peabody Award-winning American documentary producer and director. Lynda and Ann quickly became fast friends and went on to become collaborators on multiple projects. At this same party, Ann also met her future husband, Carl Sagan. That's quite a party!

Super Connectors: Introverts or Extroverts?

At this point, you might be wondering if all Superhosts (and by extension, all Super Connectors) are "extra-extroverted" like our friend Nora Paxton. The short and definitive answer here is "no."

Super Connectors, including Superhosts, can be *either* introverted *or* extroverted.

There are pros and cons to each personality type when it comes to being a Super Connector. For example, while extroverts might naturally meet a lot of people, introverts tend to make fewer but deeper connections. If the extrovert is the life of the party and can bring people together, introverts are more likely to make great connections *among* the attendees and help them bond with each other.

The best Super Connectors bring the strengths of both extroverts and introverts to their relationships. If they are naturally extroverted, then they adapt to listen and observe more, and from there, connect people with each other based on their shared interests or values. If they are naturally introverted, then they learn to be much more outgoing, gregarious, and social, and thereby to attract and draw people together to an event. As a result, Super Connectors can often be described as being *ambiverts*.

To be fair, there are some archetypes where being an extrovert or an introvert can be an advantage. It would seem, for example, that it's easier to be a Superhost if you're an extrovert, as is Nora Paxton. As we'll see later, many of the Seer archetypes I've interviewed tend to be more introverted, as that gives them an opportunity to observe, listen, and process what they are seeing. One's introversion or extroversion, however, is not the defining characteristic of any Super Connector archetype; merely one of several factors that play a role in their effectiveness and approach.

The next story is an example of an introverted Superhost. This story also demonstrates how you don't need a literal *hearth*, meaning a fire or a fireplace, to be a Superhost. Superhosts can create a sense of *home, hearth, and hygge* even around a hole in an icy lake in Milwaukee in the middle of winter.

Nick Garbis

December 27, 2020, was a cold Sunday in Minneapolis, with midday temperatures at about twenty-one degrees Fahrenheit. Nick Garbis was going through a very difficult time in his life. He was in the middle of a divorce and living alone. It was also the first year of the COVID-19 pandemic, so like millions of others, he was isolated, unable to spend time with his family and friends. To top it off, it was Christmas season, which made his isolation and loneliness that much worse.

One morning, Nick and a friend walked onto Lake Harriet, which was frozen solid at the time, and trudged their way to a spot where Nick had cut out a hole two days before. The hole was about eleven feet by eleven feet. Nick had put fencing around the hole for safety to help keep people out. The hole had since frozen over, so using saws they had brought, they cut out the hole again. They cut out a piece of ice, put it off to the side, cut another piece, put that one aside, and so on, until the hole was restored.

Then, Nick and his buddy stripped down to their shorts, dove into the freezing water, and swam.

They were not in the water for very long, a few minutes at most, but they returned the next day, and the day after that. "For two weeks, we went every day, sometimes twice a day," he shared. After a while, a couple of their other friends joined them, and the four of them went regularly. It was a great way for them to meet up and socialize in a safe way during the pandemic. They reveled in the brisk icy swim, and in the easy camaraderie that followed as they shared a warm breakfast at a restaurant afterward.

Two years later, Nick now has a community of hundreds of friends who do this with him at Lake Harriet. Many are people Nick had not known before, but have since become fast friends. They are people from all walks of life, different races, age groups, sizes, colors, political affiliations, you name it. The one thing they all have in common is they love to swim in this icy lake in the middle of winter.

So how did Nick create a sense of *home, hearth, and hygge* in the middle of an icy lake, in the middle of winter in Minneapolis, during the COVID-19 pandemic to make hundreds of new friends?

When I asked Nick how this happened, he explained how this was not his goal when he started. It began simply as a way for him to get together with his three friends. Over time, more of their friends joined, and then eventually even strangers participated. Nick explained: "There's a walking path around the lake, so there's a lot of visibility to the public. One weekend, there were four of us in the water, but maybe twenty-five observers around the lake. It was like a zoo, a Sea World or something. People would come over and ask what we're doing and why we're doing it. I just told them why I love it."

He would explain how cold water swimming is good for you. There are many studies that corroborate this, and the benefits include: (1) a boost to your immune system, (2) improved circulation, (3) reduced stress, (4) burning calories, and even (5) increased libido. According to IPRS Health, "Cold water swimming activates endorphins. This chemical is what the brain produces to make us feel good during activities. Cold water swimming is also a form of exercise, and exercise has been proven to treat depression. Cold water swimming brings us close to the pain barrier. Endorphins are released when we're in pain, to help us cope with it."

What made people want to *try* was seeing Nick and his friends having fun in the water; but what made them *come back* was the sense of *home, hearth, and Hygge* they experienced. So, what did Nick and his friends do to create this experience?

First, they very consciously made everyone feel welcome and at *home*. "We're very inclusive and non-judgmental, and as a result, it's a very loving place," Nick explained. The swim is open to anyone who wants to try it, and there are no expectations about how to do it. Nick sets the example by being authentic, leaning into what he calls *fuckery*, taking cannonball dives and generally goofing around with his friends.

They also focus on creating and tending to the *hearth*, which in this case is the hole in the ice and the area around it. They treat everyone's safety and well-being very seriously, and they take the time and make the effort to prepare the area for the swim. Nick noted how there is a sense of shared experience and ritual in the preparations, with the communal work of cutting a hole in the ice, lifting up and stacking the pieces of ice to the side, setting up the fence around the hole, keeping the area clean and safe, and so on. During the pandemic, they made sure that everyone was masked and tested for COVID-19.

All of this engenders a sense of *hygge* for the participants. "It's almost like a religious experience," he said. The sense of communal well-being is engendered in the shared ritual of creating this safe space in the middle of an icy lake, by sharing a place where people of all backgrounds can come and just be themselves, and by simply enjoying each other's company. "If you don't go for a while," Nick observed, "your whole being suffers!"

Nick remembers feeling like he did not belong anywhere when he was growing up. His family was loving but also full of tension, which was hard for Nick. At school, he was never one of the "cool" kids. "I didn't have the latest fashionable clothes or shoes, and I wasn't all that good at sports." He had a hodgepodge of multicultural friends around him, "mostly first or second generation immigrants like me from Irish, Greek, Italian, Polish, and Jewish families," other kids who also felt like they did not belong who found solace with each other.

Even as a young adult, while he had lots of colleagues and friends around him, Nick rarely, truly felt at home. That is, until he cut open a hole in the middle of a frozen lake in Minneapolis and became a Superhost for others to join him. For his fiftieth birthday, on Feb 22, 2021, he and a few hundred of his friends celebrated at the lake. He dressed up as a pirate, and as he told it, "a lot of tomfoolery ensued."

Superhost Best Practices

In the next chapter, we'll consider what happens when Super Connectors go beyond creating a sense of welcome for groups of people to create a *community* where there are many connections among the members, and the relationships (and the community) persist beyond the Super Connector. First, however, we'll conclude this chapter with a few tips from Superhosts on how to become better at being a Superhost:

1. Be Genuine

People relate to you for who you are. Don't throw a dinner party if that's not you, maybe host a poker night instead. Certainly don't carve out a hole in the middle of a frozen lake if you're not into cold water immersion. Find the activity that makes you happy, and share it with others.

2. Be Consistent

The best-selling author and community building expert, Charles Vogl, writes about how he and his wife hosted hundreds of dinner parties on Friday evenings over the years when he was studying at Yale. It was hard work, and at times barely anyone showed up. But over time, his dinners became something standard in the lives of his friends, and an event that they looked forward to attending.[4]

3. Focus on Creating a Wonderful Experience for the Attendees

This is where *home, hearth, and hygge* come in. What are the things you can do to make everyone feel welcome? What is the *hearth* for your occasion? What kind of an experience do you want to create for your guests?

4. Focus on Enabling Connections

The key is to create opportunities for the attendees to meet and connect with each other in genuine ways. Chances are, they already know you, so it's more about how they meet each other. What activities or elements will make it easier for people to connect with each other?

In short, whether it's a fireplace, a dinner table, a game of charades, or a hole in an icy lake, Superhosts bring people together to create and nurture a sense of home, hearth, and hygge. And what a gift that is! How often do you truly feel welcome and at home, enjoying the occasion and the warm camaraderie of the people around you? In a time when people feel more disconnected with one another, Superhosts offer this incredible gift where relationships can form and deepen.

Next, we'll consider what happens when Super Connectors bring people together over an extended period of time, beyond isolated events.

Chapter 3 Notes

1. See https://www.fastcompany.com/3043468/the-secrets-of-airbnb-superhosts.
2. See https://www.vulture.com/2022/06/an-oral-history-of-contact-the-movie.html.
3. More on Nora Ephron: https://www.bonappetit.com/story/long-live-dinner-parties and https://www.thestar.com/life/2012/07/03/nora_ephrons_practical_advice_on_living_well.html.
4. See *The Art of Community: Seven Principles for Belonging*, by Charles H. Vogl, Berrett-Koehler Publishers, 2016.

CHAPTER 4:
THE COMMUNITY BUILDER

"If I can change where you belong, I can change what you believe"
~ Ryan Groves ~

An interesting thing happened with Nick Garbis and his friends at Lake Harriet. We noted in the previous chapter how what started out as a small band of friends became a much larger group of a few hundred people over time. The group then took on a life of its own, and the members began to self-organize. For example, they started a chat group in the messaging app, WhatsApp, where they would text each other about when they were planning to go ice-swimming during the winter months, but also about other things going on in their lives, especially during the rest of the year. Additionally, they developed a group identity: They call themselves the *HMH Submergents* ("HMH" cheekily stands for *Harriet's Magic Hole*). They even have a logo for the group! In short, what began as Nick and his buddies hosting daily dips in the icy Lake Harriet became a self-organizing *community* of hundreds of people who support one another throughout the year, beyond any one event.

This chapter is about Community Builders, Super Connectors who build, maintain, and grow communities of people. Communities are different from an event in that communities persist over time, beyond just one or more events. An event is something that happens at a given time and location, such as a dinner party, or an icy dip in Lake Harriet. But when a group of people get together repeatedly, they can become a community, and it takes a Community Builder to make this happen.

Mike MacCombie

Take the example of Mike MacCombie, who built a community called "Open Mike Night." Living in NYC in 2015, he remembers going to various "networking" events and having other people "look past" him because he was "just a teacher" at the time. The other attendees were thinking transactionally, looking to "network" with people who are "useful" to them, such as potential investors, senior executives to sell to, people to hire, and so forth. In contrast, Mike wanted to connect with people *relationally*, and build a community of people he liked being with.

So that's what he did. Mike asked himself, "What happens if I get ten really great people together, with no goal other than just to hang out?" He then drew on his education and training in human behavior and organizations, and began Open Mike Night in 2016. He started with about ten people that he liked, and brought them together into fun gatherings with certain rules of engagement in place – just like Benjamin Franklin did with the twelve members of his Leather Apron Club!

Today, Open Mike Night is a community of *thousands* of people across multiple major cities, including New York City, San Francisco, and Los Angeles. While he does not charge the community members a fee to participate, he has had more job opportunities and deals come through this community than he can handle. More to the point, the members of this community have been able to build long-lasting, trusted relationships that have developed into all kinds of business opportunities, jobs, funding, and even deep friendships. Mike was able to create a thriving community where business stuff happened but without the "networking."

So how did he do it? What do Community Builders like Mike do to create thriving communities? If you identify as a Community Builder, how can you become better at building communities?

Importance of Communities to Super Connectors

The importance and impact of communities to *society* cannot be overstated, and is beyond the scope of this book. But in the context of Super Connectors, there are a few key points to highlight about communities.

First, communities last over time, and often live on beyond the community builder. Take the example of Benjamin Franklin and how his Leather Apron Club became the American Philosophical Society. In contrast, an event is just a single occurrence in time, and relies on the host to make it happen. This nature of communities to persist means they have an impact on its members and others around them over time, thus amplifying their impact.

Second, communities create a sense of identity and belonging for its members. Many communities adopt a name, such as Benjamin Franklin's Leather Apron Club, Nick Garbis's HMH Submergents, and Mike MacCombie's Open Mike Night. Community members identify themselves with the group *and* its other members. "I am a member" and "these are my people" are phrases indicating this sense of belonging and community identity.

Third, communities have inherent community power. Helen Keller said, "Alone we can do so little; together we can do so much," and that is exactly what I mean here. Individually, there is very little that we can do, no matter how capable we are. There is no amount of water I can shut off in my house to fight the drought problem in California. But together as a community of people, aligned toward a common goal, we can accomplish far more. While we often celebrate the achievements of individuals throughout history, the most widely impactful things have arguably been accomplished by groups of people.

Fourth, this is where Super Connectors come in. The Super Connector's power is community power, and rests in their ability to form, grow, nurture, and leverage communities. Anna Morgenstern used communities to help coach her dating clients, and Tony Leng used communities to build his network. Nora Paxton and Nick Garbis instinctively drew people around them by hosting amazing events, and as we'll see in the later chapters, all of the other Super Connector archetypes also leverage communities to do what they do. Catalysts mobilize communities toward a goal. Ambassadors connect different communities together. Seers inform communities. Elders maintain the values and integrity of communities, and so on. It's almost impossible to become a *Super* Connector without communities.

Community Builder Best Practices

Let's turn back to Mike MacCombie and other Community Builders to see how they build thriving communities.

1. Start small

Manoj Govindan, Venture Builder and Head of Strategic Partnerships at Prudential Financial and a Super Connector himself, advises Community Builders to think about "minimum viable community." What is the *minimum* number of people you need to make your community viable, and start with that.

Anecdotally, the number seems to range between ten and twelve. Mike MacCombie began Open Mike Night with just ten people for the initial meeting, and grew from there. Rebecca Friese had twelve women for her "12 at 12" luncheons. Nora Ephron invited just enough people to her dinner to fit around a large circular table (a 72-inch round table can seat up to ten adults). Benjamin Franklin started his Leather Apron Club with just twelve ingenious men.

You don't need a large group to get started, but the group must "gel" when they get together, which leads us to the next point.

2. Curate the members

Mike carefully pre-selected the attendees for his first event. He said he curates for "personality rather than their jobs." They came from a wide variety of backgrounds and roles, but they all shared something in common with each other.

There are many other examples of this kind of curation in effect. The members of Benjamin Franklin's club were all enterprising tradesmen whom he respected for their industriousness and intellect. David Homan, a Super Connector of Super Connectors, carefully vets everyone he invites into his community called Orchestrated Connecting. His criterion: "Do I trust this person to watch my kids for several hours?" You'll learn more about David and his network later in the book. Zem Joachin spends an hour rigorously interviewing each person before she invites them to her 250-person annual event called the Near Future Summit. Peter Sims, the founder of the BLKSHP community of artists and entrepreneurs, is adamant that "culture fit" is the most important aspect when bringing in new members.

What is the point of all this effort to pre-select the members of the community?

First, this creates a sense of *shared identity*. The phrase *birds of a feather* is apt here. The *feather* can be as simple as a shared activity, such as wanting to swim in an icy lake in the middle of winter. Or it can be professional, such as when Yousuf Khan (mentioned in Chapter 3) gathers his CIO friends together for his monthly events. Either way, the selection helps to ensure that when the participants show up, they know they are among a group of people with whom they share something important in common.

Second, the vetting *increases trust*. Being with others with whom you share something important in common instills trust to some degree. But knowing that every participant has been vetted for trustworthiness, that's something else. Knowing that Dave Homan trusts everyone in the group with the safety of his children envelops the whole community in an umbrella of trust in the most sacred sense. Knowing that Peter Sims has vetted everyone for their "inner artist" creates a fantastic environment where people can feel safe and let themselves be creative.

Third, the shared identity and high trust create a foundation for the community to *grow*. The people who are invited find in the community a sense of belonging with one another, and an environment of high trust, which make them want to remain in the community. They will then often invite or recommend their friends to join, and over time, others who were not invited are also drawn to the community for all that it offers to its members.

And this growth is important for the health of the community. There has to be some level of growth, with new members and activities, for the community to be healthy. And in order for the community to grow, the Community Builder has to employ two other best practices.

3. Create the *structures* for the members to connect with each other

This is critical. For a group of people to become a *community* and last beyond the founder, the members have to be able to connect and get to know each other *without* the Community Builder. Otherwise, the community will be limited in scale to the energy and capacity of the Community Builder. What distinguishes the Community Builder from the Superhost is that the former focuses on the *structure* of the community itself to help members to connect with each other, while the latter focuses on the event (where he or she is present).

So how do Community Builders do this? Below are some examples.

One, they establish clear guidelines and rules for how the community operates. How often do you meet, and where? What time does it start and end? Who "runs" the meetings and what is the purpose of the gathering? How do you communicate in between the meetings? And what are the "rules of engagement" when you meet? For example, Mike MacCombie has just four simple rules for his Open Mike Night events:

1. No flaking. If someone is running late or can't make it, they have to communicate with the organizer proactively.
2. No networking and no business cards. You were not allowed to "network" and ask what people do for a living, or to talk about what you do for a living. It was much more about who people are as people, not their jobs or careers.

3. Treat people with respect regardless of their context. Mike adds, "Everyone is positive, and has a positive outlook on life. They are pleasant toward others, regardless of the context. They are generous, and open-minded to new experiences."
4. Something happens at 7:00 pm at every meeting.

These guidelines and rules create the structures and norms around which the members of the community can congregate and connect with each other on a regular, on-going basis, without having to "reinvent the wheel" every time.

Second, the Community Builders leverage other Super Connectors to help scale the community. The Superhost can help by hosting local events. The Catalyst helps to align and drive the community toward a shared goal. The Advocate highlights and advocates for specific individuals who can help the community. The Seer informs the community with new insights. The Ambassador brings multiple communities together. The Elder helps maintain the values and culture of the community, and so forth. And other Community Builders can help create additional chapters of the community. The Community Builder is aware of these other Super Connectors in the community (often instinctively), and will work with them to help the community grow and thrive.

Third, Community Builders use tools to help the community to connect and grow. How the members of HMH Submergents use WhatsApp to communicate with each other is a great example. Many communities will have their own websites for their members, or a membership group on social media. Many also send out regular newsletters or emails to keep its members informed of the latest developments in the community, the arrival of new members, new insights, and so forth.

4. Add differentiated value to the community members

The community has to add value beyond the relationships – what I call differentiated value. The relationships are foundational to the community, but for the members to continue to participate, there has to be some kind of value that they get from their on-going participation. That can be vocational (e.g. I am getting better at my profession because of this community), or for a hobby (e.g. such as ice water swimming), or for a greater purpose (e.g. I am helping to clean up our oceans). Whatever it is, the members have to get value beyond the relationships for the community to grow and thrive.

This leads us to the next archetype, the Catalyst. But before we go there, let's take a look at another example of a Community Builder, one where the question of "value" is central to her role. Put another way, can you create enough value in a community to make a living as a Community Builder?

This is relevant because many Super Connectors I've met have struggled with this question: how can I make a sustainable living from doing what I love to do as a Super Connector? Connecting people is by definition "social," and when you make it "transactional" by charging for it, you run the risk of ruining the social element. For every Super Connector archetype, there are jobs that are well-suited for that type (for example, executive recruiters for Matchmakers). This is an example of a professional Community Builder who operates at an exceptional level.

Vanessa DiMauro

If you're looking for examples of people who build and manage communities for a living, the name Vanessa DiMauro will often come up at the top of your search results. After all, she's been doing this for more than twenty years! There are others like her, many of whom I'm grateful to call friends, such as Gamiel Gran at Mayfield Ventures, Rob Simms at Cisco, Bob Bierman at the G100, Ray Wang at Constellation Research, Frank Bell at InspireCIO, Heidi Messer at Collective-i, Wendy Howell at the Executive Council Network, Dan Fitzpatrick at Dell Ventures, and Dave Best at SustainableIT.org, among others. Like them, Vanessa is an expert, and has worked over the years with thousands of senior executives as her clients and community members. Here is her story:

Vanessa grew up in a small town in the middle of Connecticut called Rocky Hill. Her parents were both in the travel industry. Her father led a travel agency that took thousands of people on various trips around the world, and her mother worked as a flight attendant. As a result, Vanessa and her sister got to travel all over the world as they were growing up, experiencing different cultures, peoples, languages, foods, and norms. She credits her ability to cross social boundaries to her many travels with her parents. For Vanessa and her family, there was nothing "weird" about anyone they met, or with anything they saw; they just accepted that this was how people and things were in the world, be it their language, food, clothing, or custom.

Vanessa displayed her natural talents as a Community Builder in high school. As she told it, "My sister was the prettiest and the most popular, but I won 'best community builder' because I just *ran* things. I ran the yearbook, I was president of the tennis club, and so forth."

She emphasized that she did so simply because she wanted to *help* her friends and not because she wanted attention or credit for herself. To this day, she is reticent about drawing attention to herself, even professionally. She prefers to work behind the scenes by creating a platform where her community members can thrive. "My whole reason for existing professionally is to be the 'guide on the side, not the sage on stage,'" she explained. "My joy comes from, and my fulfillment comes from, empowering others."

Because of her efforts and her natural ability to lead, she was very popular with her peers, and she always felt like she belonged. You might recall that some of the other Super Connectors I mentioned earlier, including Anna Morgenstern, Tony Leng, Nora Paxton, and Mike MacCombie, experienced a sense of dislocation, of *not* belonging. Vanessa's example shows how one does not have to go through a sense of dislocation or feeling unwelcome to want to create a community. For Super Connectors, it's a natural desire they all share to want to help others by connecting people and welcoming them into communities. Vanessa shared, "When you're popular like I was, it can go one of two ways: You can be the mean girl, or you can be the one who welcomes everybody. I welcomed everybody."

After graduating from Boston College with a degree in English, she ended up working for a government-funded think tank called Technical Education Research Center (TERC) where she really got into community building professionally. Since then, and over the course of more than twenty years, she has worked with thousands of leaders around the world in dozens of executive communities. In fact, she has personally built five executive communities herself, and has sold two of them. Today, she is the Head of Community at a venture capital firm called Georgian Ventures.

She and the others I mentioned earlier (such as Gamiel Gran, Wendy Howell, Dan Fitzpatrick, Heidi Messer, and Ray Wang) are all examples of Super Connectors who thrive as professional Community Builders. What they do and how they do it could fill another book. For now, I'll end this section with this anecdote from Vanessa, one that illustrates the value that her community members get, in addition to the relationships.

She currently runs a community for the CEOs of Georgian Ventures' portfolio companies. During COVID, these entrepreneurs all struggled to deal with the crisis brought on by the pandemic. As she told it:

"The world was going to hell in a handbasket. They were doing remote layoffs, and all sorts of terrible things were happening. They were trying to figure out how to run their company while shutting parts of it down. We moved our meetings to a weekly cadence, with no agenda, just to provide a support system. So these CEOs would just come, and sometimes they would just cry. It was a really rough time, and they would support each other. And then they started telling each other these amazing things that were happening, some of it headwinds, others tailwinds. There was no playbook for how to deal with the pandemic, so they shared with each other, supported one another, and learned from each other."

She continued, "At the end of the year, we collected their amazing stories into a book that was sent only to the members. It's a collection of their stories and quotes that describes what they did during this time." The book served as a testament of the crisis they had gone through together, and how they helped one another. It was a testament to the value they all got from the community, from each other. "A lot of them were just really moved because they had gone through this crisis together, and this book captured and validated their journeys."

The entrepreneurs in this community learn from each other about how to be a better CEO, how to hire and motivate the right leaders, how to get to product-market-fit, how to secure your first set of customers, how to scale your business, and so forth. And in this case, they helped each other through a once-in-a-century global crisis in a way that was both personally and professionally meaningful. That's the kind of value that Community Builders can bring to their members.

Now, let's turn to the Catalyst, the agitator and change agent among the Super Connector archetypes. They have the power to help a community to change and grow, but in doing so, they can also disrupt the stability of the community!

CHAPTER 5:
THE CATALYST

"If you are entrusted with bringing about change, you likely possess the knowledge needed to advance the organization. But knowledge is not enough. You have to bring yourself to each interaction in a deeply authentic way. People don't care how much you know until they know how much you care."
~ Doug Conant ~

Apple Computer's innovative 1997 "Think Different" advertisement talked about change agents. You might have seen it. Steve Jobs, the late founder and CEO of the company, narrates it as follows:

> "Here's to the crazy ones. The misfits. The rebels. The troublemakers. The round pegs in the square holes. The ones who see things differently. They're not fond of rules. And they have no respect for the status quo. You can quote them, disagree with them, glorify or vilify them. About the only thing you can't do is ignore them. Because they change things. They push the human race forward. And while some may see them as the crazy ones, we see genius. Because the people who are crazy enough to think they can change the world, are the ones who do."[1]

The advertisement includes images of Albert Einstein, Bob Dylan, John Lennon, Buckminster Fuller, Thomas Edison, Muhammad Ali, Ted Turner, Maria Callas, Amelia Earhart, Alfred Hitchcock, Martha Graham, Jim Henson (with Kermit the Frog), Frank Lloyd Wright, and Pablo Picasso, among others. You might call them change agents or catalysts. And as amazing and impactful as these historical figures have been, however, they are not the ones we're talking about here in this chapter.

In the context of this book, Catalysts are Super Connectors who drive change by *connecting and leveraging other people.* They are not the lone change agents railing against the system, like some of the greats mentioned in the Apple ad. Catalysts recognize they cannot do it alone, and that instead they need lots of other people to drive that change. Their power lies in articulating the goal or mission, and then in identifying, inspiring, and connecting others to join in that mission. In the process, they make "catalytic connections" that change people's lives.

Put another way, they drive change *through* and *with* communities. As we saw in the previous chapter, Community Builders create communities where they didn't exist before, and these communities have community power. This power, however, is mostly latent, untapped. Catalysts are the Super Connectors who convert the latent, potential energy of a community into actual, kinetic energy, and it is an energy that can move mountains.

Let's take a look at a couple of examples to see what these Catalysts do and how they do it.

Ryan Groves and the Breakfast Bowtie Club

Ryan Groves is a self-described "Kansas Farm Boy" who became the founder and CEO of a nonprofit organization during college, and whose efforts were noticed by the First Lady of the US at the time, Laura Bush. This is his story.

Ryan grew up in Kansas to a family of farmers. His parents and grandparents were all farmers, raising various crops and cattle over many generations. Now, "farming" may conjure up images of the lone farmer, rugged and independent, working the land to provide for his family. What Ryan learned growing up is that "community" is critical to farming. He shared, "Starting my story with the farm in Kansas is important because you can't farm on your own. The farm next door is so critical to your success."

Ryan's appreciation for community deepened during his high school years when he bonded with a local Christian worship group of his peers. He explained how "it was not a straight-laced religious fervor group" but instead more like "a few Christian kids getting together to talk about life." They would "skip class from time to time, buy some donuts, listen to reggae music, and skate board for fun." They supported one another with their faith, school, dating, and life in general. "It was a super rad prayer group," he recalled, and one where he felt a deep sense of belonging.

When he entered college, he expected to be "surrounded by other young, idealistic people who are, like me, looking for a great group friends, a community I could belong to where we could just go on adventures together." Instead, he was very disillusioned by the "transactional, appetite-driven" nature of the people around him at school. Discouraged and lonely, he yearned for a greater sense of belonging and purpose, much as he had in high school.

Around this time, Ryan learned there was a water crisis, and that billions of people around the world didn't have access to clean water. This was when he had the idea to bring other students together to help with this cause. He thought to himself, "Maybe this is the thing I can rally people around at school. We'll get a small group or chapter together, we'll do some events, and we'll raise some money." Thus, "Wishing Well: Water for the World" was born.

It started out as a small group of friends at Oklahoma Christian University in 2006. They formed a club and began to hold events to bring awareness to the club and their cause. The name of the club was the Breakfast Bowtie Club - simply because they would meet for breakfast wearing bowties (recall that Benjamin Franklin also started with a club named the Leather Apron Club).

Ryan shared this fun example. One time, he and his club members wanted to set up an art show to bring awareness to the water crisis and their efforts. To do that, they needed to get into the Student Union building to set up the show, but it was after hours, when the building was locked. To gain access to the building, they befriended the security guard. They found out he liked to play pool, so they offered him games of pool at the local pool hall in return for access to the building after hours! The art show was a success, and the club grew from there.

When they invited others to join the club, the emphasis was on the relationships. "We want *you*, not your wallet," he explained to prospective participants. And as we talked about earlier, this focus on relationships created a powerful sense of belonging, shared identity, and ultimately, a shared belief for the club members.

Their shared belief was that they *could do something about the water crisis*. Based on that belief, they held other events, such as prayer nights, and continued to fundraise. In 2010, they partnered with Tom's Shoes for an event where 250 high school and college students "walked barefoot for two miles through downtown Oklahoma City, carrying water jugs" (according to Wikipedia). At another point, Ryan and his friends flew to Rwanda to help dig wells, raise money, and film a documentary about the water crisis. Their little club expanded, and grew into other chapters at other universities.

Their efforts eventually caught the attention of Laura Bush, the First Lady of the United States at the time. She remarked, "Clean water, it's so simple. It's something all of us can do, even college students. We can go to a village and build a water well, and we know things are going to be better than they were... Because of your generosity, hundreds of children will have access to clean water."[2]

Maybe more importantly for Ryan, he now had his community of friends with whom he could go on adventures together and share that deep sense of purpose and belonging. "That small group of friends became so close and tight," he recalled. The water crisis was a "very virtuous excuse" to create what he wanted most, that close-knit community of friends. And because he could not find it at the university, he created it and then "gave it away to others" for them to join. "I could have swapped out the water crisis with any number of causes," he noted. The key idea is "How do I belong to something? Once we have that belonging, we can do anything!"

Therein lies the key connection between communities and change. Ryan believes that if you can change where someone belongs, you can change what they believe, and if you can change what they believe, you can change how they behave. Belong → Believe → Behave.

Now let's consider what Ryan and other Catalysts do to bring people and communities together to drive change.

Catalyst Best Practices

1. Articulate a Goal or a Mission

More than any other Super Connector, the Catalyst is focused on a mission or purpose. In Ryan's case, it was about the water crisis. Peter Sims, with his BLKSHP community, focuses on revitalizing the world with artists through a movement that he calls the "New Renaissance." Adria Dunn is a Super Connector of Super Connectors whose mission is to help various nonprofits by connecting them with family offices and high net worth individuals in meaningful ways. Catalysts articulate their purpose in a way that is inspiring for other people, and then draw people around their cause.

2. Build or Leverage a Community

They know they cannot do it alone, so they leverage an existing community, or create one if none exists around them that matches their cause. Ryan, Peter, and Adria all built communities of their own to support their missions, but there are other Catalysts who partner with existing communities. In either case, because the Catalyst focuses on the mission, it helps them to find and collaborate with a Community Builder who focuses on building and growing the community.

3. Focus on Culture, Values, and Shared Beliefs

As I mentioned earlier, the Community Builder curates the members of the community around a shared set of values. The culture of the community is the sum of the shared values, beliefs, and behaviors of the community members. This becomes especially important with Catalysts. Community members often volunteer their time and effort to support the mission. Without the shared values and beliefs, there can be no collective action.

4. Make *Catalytic Connections*

Catalysts excel at making connections for other people, but for them, the reason behind the connections is to support the mission. Every time Adria Dunn connects a high net worth individual to a nonprofit, she is fulfilling her mission. Peter Sims connects artists with corporate executives so they can collaborate on artistic projects that help make the world more humane. I call these "Catalytic Connections," and they can be exceptionally powerful and meaningful.

5. Identify and enroll experts

Catalysts identify and leverage the best experts they can find from within a community to help fulfill their mission. This is akin to what a producer does for movies or Broadway shows and, in fact, producers are a great example of Catalysts. They marshall all the resources they can find to make their vision a reality, and as such, they develop a knack for identifying people's strengths and talents, and in enrolling these people around their cause.

6. Partner with other Super Connectors

Some of the experts that Catalysts will find are other Super Connectors. As I mentioned earlier, Catalysts and Community Builders can be great complements to one another. But they can also work with Advocates, who excel at identifying under-represented and under-leveraged people from within a community. Or they can work with Explorers who are great at finding unexpected or hard-to-find resources and people from other communities.

We'll learn more about the Advocate, the Explorer, and other archetypes later in this book. In the meantime, let's take a look at another example of a Catalyst, one who made it her *profession* to be a Catalyst.

Shannon Lucas and her constellation of Catalysts

Shannon Lucas is a world-class expert at being a Catalyst. She and her business partner, Tracey Lovejoy, co-founded Catalyst Constellations, an organization that identifies, brings together, and empowers Catalysts. Their tagline reads: "The world needs Catalysts who create bold and powerful change in the world. We're devoted to educating, coaching and connecting Catalysts, so they can create their dream impact." They co-authored a bestselling book about Catalysts, titled *Move Fast. Break Shit. Burn Out.* They have both been Catalysts in their careers, and now work with hundreds of other professional Catalysts. It's fair to say they know a thing or two about what it means to be a Catalyst! This is Shannon's story.

Shannon herself has a multi-disciplinary background, both personally and professionally. She studied art history and French growing up, earning a degree in art history at the American University of Paris. You might think that she then went on to work in the arts, maybe in Paris or New York City. Instead, she pivoted entirely and began her career as a *network engineer* at Microsoft. She was very successful at it, and then she made another pivot into sales, excelling as a top-performing sales engineer at T-Mobile.

She then made another pivot to the world of collaborative innovation at Vodafone, and this is where she came into her own as a Catalyst. Here are some key aspects about how Shannon operated as a Catalyst at Vodafone, and you'll see many of the best practices that we read about earlier.

1. **Articulate a mission:** As their Director of Innovation at Vodafone, her mission was to "create a company-wide methodology for innovation," which would then drive new business opportunities and company growth. This mission was given to her by the company, but she embraced it wholeheartedly and was able to bring a team together around that purpose.
2. **Build or leverage a community:** "The entire program was about building a network," Shannon recalled. She started with a small

team of eight "trouble makers" from around the world. They met with people both in and out of Vodafone, and connected people who were doing innovative work with the leaders at Vodafone who could then turn those innovations into real business opportunities. Over time, she built a network of thousands of innovators, creators, and executives around the world, and her team grew from eight to eighty, all certified in their in-house developed innovation process.

3. **Make *Catalytic Connections*:** The connections that she and her team made drove massive changes for the company. "If you reach out to executives with a credible opportunity, they'll listen. But you have to come to them with something concrete and relevant," she advised. She and her team generated over 500M€ of pipeline through co-creation workshops and streamlined, repeatable innovation methodologies.

After Vodafone, she joined Cisco to create a similar program called the Cisco Hyper-Innovation Living Labs, or CHILL for short. Their goal was to create a "Minimum Viable Ecosystem Laboratory of the world's top innovation companies to co-create the future together and catalyze new growth opportunities." She and her team networked with innovators both inside and outside Cisco, connected the dots across various innovative ideas, solutions, and business challenges, and created communities of people who would collaborate to bring these solutions to market.

She took some time off to recharge before taking on her next role as the Executive Vice President and Head of Emerging Business Unit at Ericsson. There she led a $150 million business focused on new market segments for Ericsson including the Hyperscale Cloud Players and Industrials. She and her global team "generated over $1 billion of opportunities" for Ericsson in their 5G and Internet of Things (IoT) industry solutions.

4. **Focus on Culture, Values, and Shared Beliefs:** In 2017, Shannon and her friend Tracey Lovejoy co-founded Catalyst Constellations, which brings together and supports leaders who

self-identify as "Catalysts." They hold executive retreats, webinars, and workshops, conduct research, and connect and coach others who work as change agents in their respective organizations. When they bring in new members into their community, Shannon and Tracey emphasize "culture fit" and a shared value system of wanting to support one another.

5. **Leverage Other Super Connectors:** In 2021, Shannon and Tracey partnered with Samudra, which is an ecosystem of communities of purpose, where multiple communities come together in support of their collective mission to "inform and inspire future leaders toward making the world better for everyone." There, Shannon and Tracey are able to connect and collaborate with other Super Connectors, including Superhosts who put together amazing events, Community Builders who build and run the other communities, and others.

Catalysts bring people together to drive change. But change often takes time, during which unforeseen challenges can come up, and the road ahead may not always be clear. This is where the next Super Connector archetype comes in, by offering new insights that enable the community to make course corrections as they move forward.

Chapter 5 Notes

1. See https://www.thecrazyones.it/spot-en.html.
2. See https://en.wikipedia.org/wiki/Wishing_Well:_Water_for_the_World.

CHAPTER 6:
THE SEER

"In the age of revolution it is not knowledge that produces new wealth, but insight—insight into opportunities for discontinuous innovation. You must become your own seer."
~ Gary Hamel ~

How do Communities Learn?

T his is not an idle, theoretical question. In the complex and rapidly changing world we live in, we are beset by challenges for which the solutions are not yet known. Whether it's fighting climate change, removing plastics from the ocean, or making clean water available to millions, we are still trying to figure out how to solve these problems. To do this, we need a way to discover *new insights* to these unsolved challenges.

The esteemed management consultant and author John Hagel wrote, "Learning in this context is not learning in the form of sharing existing knowledge, like in training programs. It's about learning in the form of creating entirely new knowledge that never existed before. In a rapidly changing world, this is the most valuable and necessary form of learning. In this new institutional model, this form of learning is not confined to research labs or innovation centers – it is the focus and priority of every participant in the institution."[1]

Enter the Seer. If the Catalyst is the Super Connector who brings together people to create change, then the Seer is the Super Connector who brings people together to create *new insights*. They create these new insights based on the many conversations they have with the various members of a community or communities. They connect the dots across myriad conversations, ideas, and observations, then derive new insights that would not have been possible without those relationships. They also take it a step further by bringing the community members together to help *them* see the insights collectively. This is part of what makes them Super Connectors: They connect people with the goal of helping the community to see and learn.

Eric Larsen

Let's take the case of Eric Larsen as an example. He is the President of the Advisory Board Company, which is a consulting company that works with leaders in the healthcare industry around the world. He is clearly an expert in his field. He is a leading national expert on healthcare market forces and industry transformation and has served as a trusted strategic advisor to the CEOs of health systems, payers, pharmaceutical companies, physician groups, and digital-forward startups—both domestic and international—for more than two decades. Eric is a frequent conference speaker, writes extensively on healthcare dynamics, and helps guide the work of research experts studying the future of healthcare.

So how did he become such a sought-after expert, and how is he a *Seer*? The answers begin with a question he asked himself at the beginning of his career when he worked as a salesperson: "What happens if I work 10% fewer hours?" To his surprise, he found that by working less and focusing instead on *one* thing above others, he was able to increase his sales by 30%! The following year, he doubled down on this strategy and worked 20% fewer hours, focused on that one thing above others, and was able to literally double his revenue.

What was the one thing he focused on? He focused on building long-term trusted relationships with his customers by adding value in the form of information. Instead of trying to close new deals, he focused on helping his customers with new insights. He did this partially by doing his homework and learning deeply about the industry, but he augmented that by having lots of conversations with his customers. He found that as he spoke with more of his customers, he learned more, and as he learned more, he could add more value to each conversation with new insights. Eric shared, "It's not enough to be a connector, you have to reassert and add value in every conversation." The more value he added to his customers, the more they wanted to speak with him; and the more they spoke with him, the more he learned; and the more he learned, the more value he was able to add to his customers, and so on. He created a positive reinforcing cycle of value.

Over time, he became known as *the* industry expert, the "nexus of multiple worlds" spanning across hospital systems, insurance companies, payers, private equity firms, mergers and acquisitions, and the government. He became an indispensable source of expertise and trusted insights for his clients, as well as a trusted advisor and friend who would help them with their careers by connecting them to relevant peers, pointing them toward new career opportunities, serving as a very credible reference, and so forth. Based on the strength of these trusted relationships, he was able to bring in *forty times* what the average salesperson was delivering at his company. Due to his successes, he was eventually promoted to his current role as the President of the company.

Below are some key lessons about being a Super Connector and a Seer from Eric's experiences.

First, he leaned into his strengths as a Super Connector. He explained, "I made an orthogonal decision a long time ago to focus on my strengths. Most people look at their weaknesses and try to improve them. I decided I won't apologize for my weaknesses, and I won't become a generalist. I decided instead to become world-class at a very small number of things. This freed up enormous reservoirs of energy and focus for me." For example, as he continued to excel in sales, the company wanted to make him a sales manager, but he found he didn't want to manage people, so he focused instead on what he did best, which was building trusted relationships with his customers through his insights, allowing him to close bigger deals.

Second, he has a learning mindset, not a fixed mindset. Recall how curiosity is a key attribute of all Super Connectors. His father was a technology consultant, and his mother was a real estate broker. They were both introverts, but with strong social skills and who loved to connect deeply with a small number of people. Above all, his parents prized education and nurtured a love of learning in Eric and his brothers. "It was a very intellectually curious household," he recalled. This fed and encouraged his natural curiosity and instilled in him a lifelong desire to learn.

Third, he draws from a diverse set of information sources. He observed, "My superpower is not just learning but synthesizing disparate pieces of data and turning them into actionable insights." For example, in healthcare, he speaks to both the "incumbents and disruptors." "I'm ambidextrous," he quipped, "I learn from each and cross-pollinate across the group." When he was growing up, he was encouraged to play music, so he learned to play the flute and the piano. He was also encouraged to learn multiple languages, so he learned Chinese and Japanese, eventually becoming fluent in the latter. Today, he draws on his sources from across the healthcare industry, nonprofit organizations, government agencies, and even the performing arts to help inform his understanding of the world. That diversity of perspectives is a key to his success as a Seer.

Fourth, he helps the *communities* around him with his insights. He doesn't just share what he knows through isolated, one-on-one conversations with others. He brings people together into events and communities where he shares his insights but also where they can learn from each other. For example, he speaks regularly at various industry events where he shares his insights with large numbers of people. He also hosts exclusive, by-invitation-only events for his clients where they convene in small groups to discuss the latest developments in the healthcare industry. At these events, they get to learn from each other as much as they learn from him. Either way, he is adept at generating new insights with people, and the communities around him benefit as a result.

This connection between the community and the Seer deserves emphasis. The point is that the relationship between the Seer and the community over time is essential to the success of the Seer and the well-being of the community. First, the Seer learns by speaking with various members of the community. Sure, Eric does his homework on his own, but he derives new insights by connecting the dots across the various conversations that he has. So, the community is essential to the Seer. Second, the Seer shares the new insights with the community around him. Eric doesn't keep his insights to himself but adds value by sharing them with others. This benefits the community and strengthens the relationships the Seer has with the people in the community, which then makes it easier for him to continue to engage with the community. And the impact of this value is magnified over time as the relationships deepen, trust is built, and new insights become easier to derive.

This next story helps to reinforce many of the insights from Eric's story and doubles down on the advice Eric offers us.

Rob Cross

Meet Rob Cross. Rob is currently the Edward A. Madden Professor of Global Leadership at Babson College. For nearly twenty years, he has been one of the world's leading researchers on the topic of "Organizational Network Analysis," which uses data about how people connect and collaborate at work to derive powerful, actionable insights businesses can use to be more innovative and competitive while helping employees to be happier and more effective at work. He has published multiple books on this topic, has spoken at hundreds of events, and has worked with thousands of companies to help them leverage his insights.

In our conversation, Rob noted right away how his friends tell him, "Your superpower is that you see things in situations that nobody else sees." As with Eric, it's Rob's interconnected, community-based model for deriving and sharing his insights that makes him a Seer, someone who can "see things that nobody else sees." This is his story.

Rob grew up in the 1970s as an only child to his mother and stepfather. The latter was a quality control engineer for Westinghouse, whose job had them moving up and down the East Coast of the United States "from the Panhandle of Florida to a small town in New Hampshire." As a result, Rob became accustomed to a transient life, picking up and moving from place to place and having to make new friends every couple of years. He said that while this life was difficult at times, it also taught him not to be afraid to reach out to new people and make new friends. Ultimately, it gave him the "ability to move across very different groups easily."

Rob is intensely curious, and academics came easily to him. He earned his undergraduate degree at the University of Virginia and then his MBA at the Darden Business School a few years later. After that, he went into management consulting, but during that time, he felt he "couldn't say anything that was really informative" because he was using knowledge handed down to him from others at school. Instead, he wanted to offer *new* insights and concepts to share with his clients, so he pursued and obtained his PhD from Boston University.

Now, I'd like to note here that you don't have to get a PhD to be a Seer. I've met plenty of Seers who do not have advanced degrees. What they have in common is the communal, interconnected nature of how they learn and share insights. Having said that, Rob credits his PhD for giving him not just deep domain knowledge, but the ability to see things differently. "I think the process of thinking in certain ways, with abstractions and models, is very helpful. It trains you to have the ability to just pull dimensions out, and I think that's what I do." This next part is a great illustration of that.

Toward the end of his PhD program, Rob worked for Larry Prusak, who was running IBM's Institute for Knowledge Management at the time. Rob shared, "Larry created the space for me to explore an idea that didn't have to have an immediate commercial impact." Larry gave Rob the freedom to spend a year or so interacting with the leaders of various organizations, discussing and exploring his ideas, "instead of sitting alone in a library and trying to, you know, knock out another academic paper," Rob recalled. The ideas he explored during this time ultimately led Rob to his lifelong work in Organizational Network Analysis.

The next step in his journey was to co-found a community called the Connected Commons. The Connected Commons is a research organization made up of representatives from more than 300 organizations around the world, dedicated to the collective study of how work gets done, to offer "practical strategies and structures to enable organizations and people to thrive in a connected economy." Their website adds that they are an "intentional network dedicated to developing the research, relationships, and resources that enable individuals and organizations to thrive in the Connected Economy."

At this point, we can see that there probably was a Community Builder who built and managed this community of 300+ members from around the world, as well as the hand of a Catalyst who helped to articulate the mission of this "intentional network." As their Chief Research Scientist, Rob leads their research efforts by engaging in ongoing conversations with their members to help the community come up with new insights. He is their Seer.

Let's take a step back and compare and contrast the lessons from Rob Cross and Eric Larsen.

First, Seers see through conversations. They are both clearly experts in their fields: Eric Larsen in the healthcare industry and Rob Cross in how organizations get work done. Both of them have expertise born out of ongoing conversations with a community of people. Eric continually speaks with the CEOs of hospital systems and other leaders in the industry, while Rob engages in ongoing dialog with the members of the Connected Commons. They then share back their unique insights with their respective communities.

Second, it helps to be an introvert if you're a Seer. Rob describes himself as an "extreme introvert," for example, and Eric and other Seers I've met also characterize themselves as being introverted. This is not a scientific study of the relationship between introversion and being an effective Seer, but their stories indicate that being an introvert is a helpful trait for them to be able to step back, observe, and see the larger patterns of things.

Third, Seers need time to process what they're seeing, connect the dots, and come up with new insights. According to Rob, this is especially true in the initial phases of seeing something. The larger pattern is not yet visible, so it takes Seers time to process and make sense of the data. But once they do, the new insights then come much faster. This is when they become masterful because they already have a body of knowledge to then connect the dots much faster, which leads to the next point.

Fourth, the value of the Seer is not just their knowledge, but their ability to continue offering new insights *over time*. Put another way, Seers become even more impactful and valuable over time, as their understanding of a topic deepens, along with the relationships that enable their insights. This collective wisdom of the community is not static, but is instead organic, growing and changing with the community and the times. This is when Seers become indispensable to the communities around them.

Seer Best Practices

Before we close this chapter, let's go over some of the best practices for being a Seer.

1. Have an Area of Focus

Implied in both of their stories is the fact that Eric and Rob pursued their curiosity and interest in a particular area. They were not happy with the status quo and pursued new insights in that field. And it's okay if the field does not yet have a name because then that probably means it's an area not yet well understood and is ripe for a Seer to go in and understand. Eric and Rob each had a field they focused on, and over time they became known for their expertise in that area.

2. Connect Dots Across Many Fields

Jen Snow said, "Why wouldn't you look at physics and art and music and pull all of those together in a meaningful way?" Seers do not limit their research and conversations just to one field but derive insights from a variety of sources. Eric and Rob both speak with leaders from different industries and backgrounds to help inform their work. The key to this is to find and connect with experts from different backgrounds and diverse perspectives to learn from.

3. Be Intensely Curious and Ask Questions

From an early age, Eric was taught to ask questions of anybody, and to not be afraid to express his viewpoints and engage in a discussion. This was true for Rob and for all the other Seers I've met. Their curiosity makes it easier for them to cut past social and community boundaries to connect with people of different backgrounds. Their courage in challenging assumptions and asking questions enables them to arrive at new invaluable insights that we can all benefit from. The world relies on Seers to be continually and intensely curious.

4. Look for Other Super Connectors Who Can Help

The various Super Connector archetypes we've met so far combine well to help the Seer. The Matchmaker can connect the Seer with people from different backgrounds who can help inform their research. The Superhost can help the Seer by hosting amazing events where people from different backgrounds can come together to discuss new ideas with the Seer. The Community Builder can work with the Seer to nurture a learning community over time, while the Catalyst can leverage the Seer's insights to help drive the Community toward a goal.

All of the other Super Connector archetypes that follow in the next chapters are similarly additive to one another and can help in their own unique ways. With that in mind, let's now consider a close cousin of the Seer, the Innovator.

Chapter 6 Notes

1. See https://www.johnhagel.com/learning-leaders.

CHAPTER 7:
THE INNOVATOR

"Innovation is fostered by information gathered from new connections; from insights gained by journeys into other disciplines or places; from active, collegial networks and fluid, open boundaries. Innovation arises from ongoing circles of exchange, where information is not just accumulated or stored, but created."
~ Margaret J. Wheatley, Leadership and the New Science ~

W hat do NFL mascots, blood pressure monitors, and an EKG device all have in common? They were all invented by one man, Bob Stone. What's interesting here is how Bob is not an expert in any of these fields. He played football in college, but he knew nothing about creating mascots. He was an economics major and knew nothing about blood pressure monitors nor EKG devices. Yet throughout his prolific and inventive life, he would go about creating these and other innovations in different fields. This chapter is about Super Connectors like Bob, whom I call Innovators.

The importance of innovators has been written about in countless books and articles, and there are generally two types of innovators people write about. One is the idea of the lone brilliant inventor. Think Steve Jobs, Elon Musk, Bill Gates, Jeff Bezos, Thomas Watson, Henry Ford, and so on. Whether you admire them as people or not, there can be no doubt they have brought game-changing innovations to the world. The second is the idea of "open innovation" championed by large corporations like Procter & Gamble, which have implemented platforms that allow many people from different organizations to collaborate and come up with new ideas, test prototypes, and ultimately bring new products to market. Ppen innovation is not about any one person but about having a *platform* where people can come together to co-invent.

In this chapter, we consider a third option, which is the Innovator as a Super Connector. These are the people who innovate *through and with their networks of people*. Like the Explorer archetype we'll learn about in Chapter 10, Innovators are great at exploring far outside of their domain of expertise to connect with experts in *other* fields. Like the Seer, Innovators are great at connecting the dots *across* various domains, but while the Seer comes up with new *insights*, the Innovator builds new *solutions*.

This view of Innovators goes against the idea of the lone brilliant inventor, toiling away at 10,000 different ways to make an electric light bulb, as Thomas Edison did, or like Archimedes who had a brilliant insight while taking a bath and ran outside naked shouting "Eureka!" There are undoubtedly those who are brilliant and come up with new inventions entirely on their own. Of course, most innovators collaborate with other people to come up with their inventions. What Super Connector Innovators do is reach far into their communities to find the best available experts to *facilitate* the creation of new inventions. They are the glue that makes the invention possible.

This view of Innovators is also not about the "open innovation platforms" various companies have implemented. Chances are, those platforms have Super Connectors engaged to help bring participants together, curate new insights, and develop new solutions. Instead, we can think of our Super Connector Innovators as platforms for innovation themselves in that they enable innovations to take place through their networks of people. Their innovation platform is their network of people!

Author Steve Johnson, in his book, *Where Good Ideas Come From*, asserted, "Good ideas do not – for the most part – come from inside someone's head. Instead, they come from outside – specifically from social interactions." Super Connector Innovators take this a step further by actively seeking out people to create something new.

Whether it's a new physical product, a new software application, or even a new business, Innovators leverage their vast networks of people to go from an idea to a final product or service people use.

Bob Stone

Let's now consider more of Bob Stone's story. He was born in Philadelphia in the 1950s and was the eldest of three siblings. His adoptive father was a dentist, and his mother worked as his assistant at his practice. He recalled that life was not idyllic for him and his sisters, but he had three positive influences in his life that contributed to his becoming an Innovator and Super Connector.

The first was his love for sports. He excelled in sports, playing football, basketball, and baseball as the seasons changed. He recalled, "I was part of teams made up of black, white, Hispanic, and Asian kids. In sports, you judge others by their contribution to the team. We evaluated each other, not by race or skin color, but by character and athleticism." Bob developed this Super Connector ability and mindset to "see brother, not other" and to evaluate people based on their character from his participation in sports.

The second was his fascination with technology, which began when he was six years old. As he told it, "My cousin, who was in his early teens, had a crystal radio, and I was intrigued. I was amazed that a crystal, a needle, and a few electronic parts could allow me to listen to the radio! So I did chores around the house to earn the money to buy my own crystal radio." He also remembers going to the World's Fair in New York around that time. "I was amazed to see how GM imagined the future of transportation both in personal and public transport, and AT&T showed the first video telephones." He felt that "the world would change in many beautiful ways because of innovation, and it was coming fast!"

Finally, he was strongly influenced by his maternal grandfather, whom he now sees as a Super Connector himself. Bob recalled, "Walking around Philadelphia with him, I was amazed by how many people knew and respected him. He seemed to me like he was the mayor of

Philly!" His grandfather owned one of Philadelphia's first furniture factories and wholesale showrooms. Bob shared, "He mailed out short notes to friends, family, and clients on a very regular basis. After I moved, I would receive a letter from him every week. In addition, my grandparents would entertain friends most weekends both at their home and out. He was very outgoing and friendly, often stopping to talk with friends and strangers as we walked the factory and the city. He was the union representative for the owners and was well-liked by both the laborers and the other owners."

All of these experiences would combine into a potent combination for innovation with Bob, starting with his first job out of college in 1988. One of his football friends from the University of Florida was Gene Washington, who was playing for the Minnesota Vikings at the time. He recommended that Bob apply for a job at the NFL. Bob met the President of NFL Properties, John Bello, and their CFO, John Flood, and was offered a job as the Director of Retail Licensing. "My job was to expand the quality and quantity of NFL licenses" to help broaden the appeal of the NFL and generate more revenue by licensing the NFL brand," he explained.

This was when he came up with the idea to create mascots for the entire league. When he started, only *one* team in the NFL, the Los Angeles Rams, had a mascot. He recalled, "Mary Cromwell, the wife of Rams player Nolan Cromwell, was making baby clothes with cute animal characters dressed in NFL team uniforms. She wanted to license and sell these clothes to stores. From that, I got the idea to give every team a character, a mascot."

He pitched the idea of team mascots to the VP of Retail Licensing Frank Vuono, along with John Bello and John Flood. Of course, this turned out to be a billion-dollar idea for the NFL. Now, most NFL teams have team mascots, and you can find their images on T-shirts, sweatshirts, socks, plush toys, bobblehead figures, and even seven-foot-tall inflatables. "NFL Properties became very important to the league because our revenue showed great growth year after year," Bob remarked.

Getting the various NFL teams to agree to this, however, was not an easy feat. He described it as "the most difficult job of convincing I've ever done in my life," as each of the team owners had their own agendas, ideas, and concerns. He knew he could not accomplish this on his own, and he instinctively reached out to various people to help get the idea across the finish line. In one case, for example, he won over the son of one of the team owners to support the idea and advocate for it with his father. It worked! The NFL commissioner also proved to be a key ally, as he was "very helpful in getting reluctant owners to agree."

Once he was given the green light to produce the mascots, he faced his next challenge, which was *how* to make them. Bob emphasized that he knew nothing about merchandising, design, animation, or anything else about how to actually do this. So again, he reached out to people across different fields. For example, he went to Disney, Warner Brothers, and other studios to recruit some of the best animators at the time to come work for him at the NFL. One of the folks he recruited was Art Leonardi, the animator of Pink Panther, and another was Colin Blane, who worked on Looney Tunes for Warner Brothers. "These were legends of animation back when animation cells were drawn by hand," he said.

Let's take a step back and see how Bob operated as a Super Connector Innovator here. First, there was a need (the NFL wants to merchandize its brand and increase its revenue). He didn't go into a lab and try to invent something new all by himself. He also did not create a platform or a program for others to innovate. He instead went out and found the inspiration for an idea, got the necessary buy-in from a group of very doubtful team owners, and then assembled world-class talent from different fields to make the idea into a reality. He was not an expert himself in any of the required disciplines, but he knew how to bring people together to build something new.

Note the similarities and differences between the Catalyst, the Seer, and the Innovator. The Catalyst identifies a need (e.g., the lack of clean water) and rallies a group of people to take action to help address the need. The focus here is less on expertise (though that is always helpful) and more on taking collective action. On the other hand, the Seer is constantly connecting and speaking with people, coming up with new insights for the community, which the community then uses to make more informed decisions. For the Seer, the output is insights, not inventions. For the Innovator, it's about pulling together the right experts to help build something new.

What's really powerful here is that the Innovator's power is fungible. It can be leveraged across very different fields, such as going from NFL mascots to blood pressure monitors.

Later in his career, Bob's passion for technology led him to work for Bosch, the German multinational engineering and technology company that makes automotive components, industrial products such as drives and controls, as well as other products used in homes, buildings, and hospitals. There, he built the first "cuff-less" blood pressure monitor. Traditional blood pressure monitors use "cuffs" that tighten around your arm to measure your blood pressure. That's fine when your doctor or nurse is checking your blood pressure during a routine visit, but not if you're in a hospital bed and they have to check your blood pressure regularly. Bob explained, "This can be a real pain if it wakes you up every hour while you're trying to sleep" on a hospital bed.

As before, Bob assembled a team of people to help him to build a better solution. "It's based on sensor technology and MEMS: micro-electromechanical system," he recalled. As he wasn't an expert in MEMS nor in any of the related disciplines, he found the necessary experts from various organizations including universities, competitors, and suppliers. His invention is still being used in hospitals today.

Later on still, and in a similar way, he built a better EKG device that he licensed to Johnson and Johnson. He said to me, "Remember, I'm not an engineer." In fact, he studied economics in college and holds an MBA.

His superpower in all this is his ability to innovate using the network of people around him. A few key points to note here:

First, he looks past social "differences" to connect with other people in meaningful ways. In sports, he learned that the only things that matter are the character, competence, and consistent contributions of the players. Professionally, he also connected with people from all backgrounds, focusing instead on their expertise and experiences that would be helpful to his creative goals.

Second, he is intensely curious, both about people and how things work. When he was just six years old, he was mesmerized by how a crystal radio worked, and this curiosity eventually led him to holding three patents.

Third, he is a giver, and here we can see how the giver's mentality manifests in a community of people. In short, he created a win/win situation for everyone. With the NFL, he generated enormous revenue for the NFL and the team owners, but he also provided an opportunity for everyone who worked on the project to do well while also delivering fun products for the fans to enjoy. He did not do something that benefited only him. Instead, he rallied a group of people to develop something that benefited the communities around him. Think of the good he has brought to the world with his cuff-less heart rate monitor!

Manoj Govindan

Let's now consider the story of Manoj Govindan. His background is quite different from Bob's, and he is a great example of a Super Connector Innovator who operates within a large company. But the lessons from his experiences are consistent with what we see with Bob.

Manoj grew up in southern India, in the state of Kerala, which he calls "God's own country, very lush, with a very literate population." While Bob had a difficult childhood, Manoj had a very supportive family, especially his father. His father had grown up very poor and under-educated but became a self-made and successful executive of a large multinational company. He showered Manoj with love, support, and advice, which he uses to this day. The story of Manoj as a Super Connector Innovator is really a story about his father and what he taught Manoj.

Today, Manoj is Venture Builder and Head of Strategic Partnerships at Prudential Financial. He brings together a community of people to collectively identify opportunities for new products; design, prototype, and develop the products; and deliver these new products to market with Prudential Financial. The community includes innovative vendors with expertise in specific technologies and disciplines, internal and external partners with the resources and talent to help design and build the products, and business development resources to help bring the products to market. In short, what Bob Stone did with NFL mascots, EKG devices, and blood pressure monitors, Manoj has done in a role at Prudential where he can *continually* help identify, develop, and deploy new innovations.

Let's consider this for a minute. What Bob Stone created for the NFL was a multi-billion dollar windfall. What he did with blood pressure monitors changed how healthcare is delivered for millions of patients around the world. What if you could harness this kind of power and leverage it repeatedly for an organization? That's what Manoj does at Prudential and what's possible with other Super Connector Innovators.

Innovator Best Practices

What lessons did his father impart to Manoj that enabled him to become a Super Connector Innovator? Manoj shared, "My dad did not have a formal education beyond tenth grade, mostly because he was poor. He grew up in an area that didn't have running water, electricity, things like that. He stopped his education at tenth grade because he couldn't afford to go beyond that, and he had to help make a living for the family." Nevertheless, he managed to "start with a clerical job at the lowest rung of the ladder and then went on to have a full career, retiring as the President and CEO of a multinational company." Here are some of the lessons his father shared with Manoj, lessons that had an impact on Manoj being who he is today:

1. Build Trusted, Meaningful Relationships

His father, lacking a formal education, found people to help him to learn and develop, but Manoj noted how these relationships were mutually beneficial for both his father and his mentors. His father was very intentional about cultivating relationships with people who had the expertise he lacked, and in finding ways to add value while he learned from them. Similarly, Manoj cultivates relationships with experts he needs for his role at Prudential, and he makes sure these relationships are win/win for everyone.

His father also encouraged him to be curious about people and taught him how to remember details about people. "I used to be amazed at how he remembered all kinds of details about the people around him and their lives, seemingly without even trying." Manoj would hear his father speaking with people, saying things like, "How did your son's fracture on his arm turn out?" or "How was your mother's trip to the pilgrimage?" His father explained how he had a mental model, a "metadata" model, for recalling details about people and used it to help build relationships.

2. Develop Emotional Intelligence

His father helped Manoj develop high emotional intelligence. For one, he intentionally moved his family from city to city every two years. This forced Manoj to adapt to new circumstances. "Every two years, I would be faced with a new school, new friends, new neighborhood, new everything. My dad didn't have to do it. He just chose to do it." This helped Manoj to develop what he calls "anti-fragility." He explained, "Anti-fragility is not just robustness, and not just resiliency, but the tendency to actually thrive when you have challenges put in front of you. Faced with a challenge, instead of rebounding or resisting, you *thrive*."

His father also taught him to be highly empathetic. "While I was in high school, I got a call one day from my principal's office. She called me into the office, my parents were there, I didn't know why, but it turned out that they had already talked. My principal wanted to find someone from the school to be a friend and peer mentor to another student with a learning disability due to Down Syndrome." His parents had volunteered Manoj for this role! So he spent the next two years, two hours each day, with this student, learning about her, her life, her disability, and how to communicate through the limitations of her disability. In the process, he learned to be even more empathetic, to genuinely connect with people, to respect other human beings as they are, and to find common ground regardless of outward differences.

3. Build (or Leverage) Thriving Communities

His father taught Manoj about having a "feedback loop" in the communities around him. It's not enough that the people in the network are connected to each other. Something has to keep moving between the members of the network for the community to thrive. "What is the frequency, the fluency, the articulation, the simplicity, and the comprehension of feedback that is going on between the nodes in the network?" These are the interactions, conversations, exchange of insights, and collaboration towards a goal that the various Super Connector archetypes enable within a community.

4. Finding Solutions to Problems

His father also encouraged Manoj to get a degree in engineering so he could learn to think like an engineer. Manoj's explanation here emphasizes what it means to be an Innovator. "It's not about me being an engineer and coding or building something. Instead, you're looking at a problem in the world around you, and you're looking for the opportunity where I can add value." For him and other Innovators like him, the incredible value they bring is in identifying the solution and being the Super Connector who brings other people together to build it.

Now, you might have noticed that the Catalyst, the Seer, and the Innovator all need various people with specific backgrounds, experiences, expertise, and perspectives to help them with their work. But finding such people in a large community is not easy and can be time consuming. This is where the Advocate comes in.

CHAPTER 8:
THE ADVOCATE

"I have always been very proud of my Jewish heritage, which has greatly influenced my music, my worldview, and my work as an advocate for individuals whom society often leaves behind."
~ Itzhak Perlman ~

What is the difference between an Advocate and a promoter? This was the discussion I had with Arabella DeLucco that led to a deeper understanding of the Advocate archetype. "I am not a promoter!" she insisted when we spoke about her career and what she does to help people. She is the founder and CEO of WeXL, a 501(c)3 nonprofit organization based in San Francisco whose mission is to "empower underserved communities through the creative process with an impact network of leaders in arts, media, and technology." Through WeXL, and even before that, Arabella has been helping under-represented individuals within a community by interviewing them and then telling their stories through podcasts, webinars, short films, and so on.

So, how is this different from being a promoter? The word "promoter" might remind you of people like Don King, who has worked with legendary boxers like Muhammad Ali, Joe Frazier, and George Foreman, among others. Or it might bring up images of Jerry Maguire, the sports agent character played by Tom Cruise in the 1996 movie by the same name. Both Don King and Jerry Maguire are promoters for certain special individuals, be it Muhammed Ali or the fictional Rod Tidwell. But they do so commercially, for their own personal gain and that of the person being promoted (and in some negative cases, you can argue, at the expense of the person being promoted).

An Advocate is someone who highlights and "promotes" another person in a community, but does so in a way where (1) the person being advocated for benefits from the increased exposure to others; (2) the community benefits from knowing about and connecting with that individual; (3) the actions serve a greater good; and (4) there is an overall increased sense of belonging in the community as a result. Let's look at Arabella's story to illustrate.

Arabella DeLucco

Arabella and her family immigrated from the Philippines to the United States when she was five years old. As often happens with immigrants, Arrabella felt a strong sense of being "different" from her peers, and longed to simply fit in and belong in her new home. "I wanted to be an American woman and have an American experience," she recalled.

But instead of changing herself to fit in, she helped others to feel that *they* belonged. For example, when she attended Rutgers University for her undergraduate degree, she became the co-VP of Recruiting at a sorority. In this role, she sought out and recruited a diverse set of women from a variety of backgrounds, welcoming them into the community. She remarked, "I loved helping people to feel like they belonged," just as she wanted to feel when she was growing up.

After college, she held a variety of jobs, including managing online content for the Orange County Register, booking speakers for TechWeek (a popular technology publication), working on content and product marketing for technology companies, and ultimately being the CEO of her own media company where she and her team produced video content for their clients. Through this journey, she learned that one of the things she loves to do is interviewing people. She started interviewing people and sharing their stories online in 2007 when she was the CEO, Producer, and on-camera talent for her own media agency, and she absolutely loved it. "I learned that I can interview anyone," she shared.

She also learned that she loves to tell stories, and especially stories about underrepresented people with skills and experiences she thinks the community would benefit from hearing about.

For example, at WeXL, she profiled an all-male vocal group called Next Town Down. In the video titled "A Brotherhood To Success With Next Town Down," she shared the story of how five young black men who love music came together to form the band." The band members were inspired by other musicians like Khalid and SZA who were "making platinum records in their bedroom," to pursue their craft on their own without help from the "big machines or labels." To make it on their own, they were "prepared to work fifty times harder for half the results."

More than that, they *connected* with other musicians from a variety of backgrounds to expand their music and their audience. For example, they collaborated with the Filharmonic, an LA-based a cappella group of Filipino-American young men, to produce a medley honoring Justin Timberlake. Malik Knighten, one of the founding members of Next Town Down, shared, "Music, for me, was a way to just connect with other people that I didn't know, and it helped me branch out and meet new people."

And this is where Arabella helps as an Advocate. She shares their stories with her community using her videos and podcasts, but she doesn't stop there. She also actively connects them with specific community members to help them be more successful. More broadly, she created the WeXL Impact Network (WIN) to connect various community members with each other so they can collaborate and support one another in their respective endeavors. By telling their stories and connecting them with each other, Arabella is an Advocate for the people she works with.

Advocate Best Practices

So, how is Arabella's story different from that of Jerry Maguire or Don King? How are Advocates different from promoters, and what are their best practices?

1. Bringing Value to a Community, Not Just an Individual

First, the Advocate creates value for both the person being promoted and the communities they're a part of. It's a win/win. In the earlier example, the band New Town Down benefited from greater exposure and access to more listeners and collaborators. Meanwhile, the community benefited by learning about how the band approached their work, such as going it alone without a big record label and collaborating with other bands. Don King may have provided financial opportunities and fame for the athletes he represented, but how did it benefit the communities around them beyond the entertainment?

2. Being Purpose-Driven, Not Just Profit-Driven

The Advocate also does so in service of a larger purpose beyond the people and the profit involved. For example, Arabella's higher purpose is to help create a more equitable, diverse, and inclusive world. She does this by promoting under-represented minorities in order to give them more voice and opportunities for growth. I'm not saying there is anything inherently wrong in seeking to make a profit from promoting an athlete or a musical band. But as I mentioned earlier, one of the core traits of Super Connectors, including the Advocate, is being purpose-driven, and that benefits a much broader set of people!

3. Create a Sense of Belonging

Finally, but certainly not least, Arabella creates a greater sense of belonging for those whom she interviews and highlights. When Don King promotes a boxer to superstardom, does the star experience a sense of belonging? I would argue the opposite is true. The athlete is placed on a pedestal, loved or vilified, sought after, or jeered at, but ultimately winds up feeling isolated inside of their fame and fortune. Arabella promotes under-represented minorities to connect them with others such that they experience more kinship and belonging. She highlights their unique skills and value to the community so other members of the community can connect and collaborate with them, further enhancing their sense of belonging. This may be the most powerful thing the Advocate does: creating a sense of belonging by highlighting the individual as a valuable member of the community.

This is where things start to get really interesting.

What happens when an Advocate collaborates with a Community Builder? The result can be a more inclusive and cohesive community! The Advocate identifies and highlights people within the community to help create a greater sense of belonging and greater cohesion within the community. The Community Builder can leverage the Advocate to identify people who are needed for the community and help strengthen the community. As the community continues to grow, the Advocate has more people she can identify and promote within the community. The result is a virtuous cycle of growth and belonging.

What happens when an Advocate collaborates with a Catalyst? Recall that Catalysts are Super Connectors who drive change by connecting and leveraging other people, but how do they know where to find the people necessary to achieve their mission? It's difficult, even for Catalysts, to know everyone they might need, despite how connected they are. Here, the Advocate is a natural complement to the Catalyst to help identify the best people with the right skills to get the job done.

This is not about finding the most experienced people everyone looks up to as the subject matter experts or the most senior people in positions of authority and power. Those are people who are already well known in the community and are overloaded from it because of their expertise, position, and visibility. Instead, this is about finding the under-represented, undiscovered, and/or underleveraged talent inside the community with a unique set of skills who can help the community thrive and grow by applying their talents and energies to the right endeavors.

Similarly, when an Advocate collaborates with a Seer, Innovator, Superhost, or any of the other archetypes, she amplifies the others' efforts. More broadly, this is true of all Super Connector archetypes: when they collaborate, they amplify each others' efforts.

What traits and skills do you need to be an excellent Advocate? Once again, the core Super Connector traits apply here:

Trust Builders: Advocates have earned the trust of the people whom they want to highlight. At the same time, they have earned the trust of the community, based on the value they have already brought to the community through the people they have highlighted.

Curious: Their curiosity about people leads them to explore the community, meet different people, find out what makes them special, and then highlight them.

Givers: Advocating for others is a labor of love for the individuals and the community. Imagine the effort it takes to do this, and most of the time, there are no tangible, immediate benefits for the Advocate.

Purpose Driven: It's not enough to just be curious. Being curious, a Super Connector can meet a lot of people, but that can simply turn into a large group of people they happen to know. Their purpose narrows the focus of the Advocate's connections and deepens their relationships with their connections.

Moreover, the Advocate brings a unique skill to this archetype: storytelling. It can be a podcast, or a YouTube video, or a blog post, but whatever the medium, the Advocate is able to tell great, memorable stories highlighting specific individuals and their skills and value to the community.

Lorine Pendleton

Now let's consider the story of Lorine Pendleton to better understand the Advocate archetype. Marie Claire magazine named Lorine as one of the "Most 50 Connected Women in America." She is a venture capitalist and angel investor with a background as an entertainment lawyer and entrepreneur.

Lorine was born and raised in Harlem, New York, with two brothers, one older and one younger. Her parents were both native Harlemites and married when they were both eighteen, and her mother was pregnant with Lorine's older brother. Her father was determined to create a better life for himself and his family, so while working at the Brooklyn Navy Yard during the day, he went to City College at night to study engineering. He eventually received his master's degree in engineering from NYU. After graduating, he first worked at IBM and then at ExxonMobil, rising to senior leadership roles and going on to have a successful career.

Her hard working father instilled in Lorine a wonder about the world, starting from when she was just seven years old. While they were too poor at the time to travel outside of Harlem (let alone the country), he made Lorine read *Time* magazine cover to cover, often quizzing her afterward about what she read. She recalled, "We traveled a little bit, but I didn't know about the big world beyond me. And I think his doing that actually created my interest in travel and learning about the world beyond my environment, which was predominantly black and Harlem at the time. I got to see a different world through those *Time* magazines. And then we would talk about it together, so that was his gift to me."

As her father's career progressed, her parents made the fateful decision to move out of Harlem to Teaneck, New Jersey. Harlem was "really rough" at the time, and crack had just come into the area. Her parents didn't want their kids living in such an environment. Teaneck was a stark contrast. She explained, "In Harlem, all my friends were black, and I went to a black school, so all my schoolmates were also black. And then I moved to Teaneck, which was so diverse! On my block, my next-door neighbors were Jewish, we had a Jordanian family, there were two other families that were Chinese, and so forth. Many of the kids in the neighborhood were first-generation immigrants. And none of that mattered! We all got along and played together, so that was really different for me and really great!"

When she attended Brown University for her undergraduate degree, she loved experiencing even greater diversity. "Brown was Teaneck supersized in terms of diversity, with just all kinds of people from all around the world." She thrived in this environment, excelling academically, getting involved with the university community, and so on.

What she appreciated most at Brown was the opportunity to connect with people from various backgrounds. "Obviously, the education was superior and amazing. But what I got out of it is connecting with people. Diversity was always really important for me, being around different people. And while I may not initially know a lot about someone's culture, I listen, and I try to be empathetic and find the commonality."

After she graduated from Brown, she put her academic chops to good use and went to school in the evening while working a full-time job during the day, as her father had done, earning her law degree from the prestigious NYU School of Law. She then went on to have a thriving career as an entertainment lawyer, representing the likes of Prince, Chaka Khan, and Stevie Wonder at the law firm of Londell McMillan.

Then, after nearly twenty years as a lawyer and director of business development at various law firms, she switched careers to investing in startups founded by minority entrepreneurs. "About eight years ago," she recalled, "I decided I wanted to start investing in diverse and women-led companies because these entrepreneurs don't get the level of funding that startups receive from traditional venture capitalists." She noted, for example, how "only 1 percent of venture capital dollars go to African American founders." Similarly, a recent study reported in the Morningstar Investor found that in 2022, women founders received a mere 2% of the total venture capital funding in the US.[1]

Observing that "talent is equally distributed, opportunity is not," she turned all of her skills, experiences, and relationships to help the underrepresented to be more successful. "I wanted to find the most amazing entrepreneurs who have great ideas and help get funding to them." In other words, she went from working with superstar musicians and corporate clients with deep pockets to identifying and *advocating* for underrepresented entrepreneurs.

As an angel investor and Super Connector Advocate, Lorine looks for the following traits of successful entrepreneurs:

First, "it's all about the team," she said, where she looks for resiliency. "Entrepreneurs will face a lot of rejections along the way, and on top of that, the market might shift, and they have to pivot. So it's important as an entrepreneur to have resiliency and to be relentless."

Second, they need to be experts in the field, expert enough to be able to attract others to join the team. A well-known adage applies here: B players recruit C players, while A players recruit other A players.

Finally, entrepreneurs have to be sellers. They are constantly selling to investors, partners, customers, employees, and others. They are selling not just their products and services, but also their vision, and ultimately themselves.

She recalled one entrepreneur who was passionate about showing a more vibrant side of Africa to the rest of the world, demonstrating it's not just poverty, orphanages, and wars. Her startup was about creating curated travel experiences for people. Her clients included celebrities, but most were travelers who wanted to have rich, deep cultural experiences of Africa. When she heard the pitch, Lorine recalled thinking, "This is incredible. What she's doing is incredible, and people need to know what she's doing. And she needs to be supported." This is how an Advocate thinks: "People need to know what she's doing, and she needs to be supported!"

Another example from her portfolio of startups is MoCaFi, which stands for Mobility, Capital, and Finance. This startup was founded by Wole Coaxum, a former managing director at JP Morgan Chase, who is African American. Lorine noted he had been making several million dollars a year as a successful senior executive at the bank when he decided to walk away to start this company to serve a greater purpose.

Wole had learned that eighty-eight million people, mostly minorities, are "underbanked" in the United States. According to Wikipedia, "the underbanked is a characteristic describing people or organizations who do not have sufficient access to mainstream financial services and products typically offered by retail banks, and are thus often deprived of banking services such as credit cards or loans."[2] Lorine added, "There is a statistic that an African American person in the US will spend an average of $44,000 more on financial services in their lifetime than their white counterparts" due to the fees associated with check cashing, money orders, and other predatory services targeting the underbanked.

According to their website, MoCaFi "is a turnkey fintech platform for government and philanthropic organizations to provide individuals and families with cash assistance, mobile banking, and financial programming that create pathways to wealth."[3] They work with "municipalities, financial institutions, community-based organizations, and private companies to create scalable, sustainable, low-fee infrastructure for financial inclusion at the consumer-level." For example, they worked with the City of Los Angeles to "launch Angeleno Connect, a digital platform to provide residents with contactless access to cash benefits, city services, and a low-fee mobile banking account," impacting the lives of 16,000 families in the LA area. They are also partnering with the City of Birmingham "to disburse Emergency Rental Assistance Program (ERAP) funding to assist residents unable to pay rent or utilities in the aftermath of the pandemic," helping 3,000 struggling families to gain access to the funding they needed.

Lorine's investment thesis is simple: "There are great companies out there led by minorities that the traditional venture capital companies overlook." They need not only financial capital but also social capital.

Noting how venture capital is a "relationship business," she leverages her powers as a Super Connector to advocate for her entrepreneurs, and to connect them with potential customers, partners, employees, experts, and other investors to help them to be more successful. In short, she uses her network to *advocate* for these under-represented and under-resourced entrepreneurs, in service of the greater good. This is what Advocates do for the people around them.

We now turn to the Super Connector archetype who advocates not just for an individual, but for entire communities of people: the Ambassador.

Chapter 8 Notes

1. See https://www.morningstar.com/alternative-investments/women-founders-get-2-venture-capital-funding-us.
2. See https://en.wikipedia.org/wiki/Underbanked.
3. See https://www.mocafi.com.

CHAPTER 9:
THE AMBASSADOR

"Unfortunately the world is what it is now. People don't get along for whatever reason. As professional athletes, in a way we're almost ambassadors for peace, because sports brings everyone together."
~ Venus Williams ~

When Abraham Lincoln was inaugurated as the President of the United States on March 4, 1861, the nation was on the brink of a civil war. The democratic union created less than a century ago was about to be torn apart. In his speech, President Lincoln asked this of his fellow country men and women: "Though passion may have strained, it must not break our bonds of affection. The mystic chords of memory, stretching from every battlefield and patriot grave, to every living heart and hearthstone, all over this broad land, will yet swell the chorus of the Union, when again touched, as surely they will be, by the better angels of our nature."[1]

Unfortunately, the people did not listen, and on April 12, 1861, the Civil War broke out. As the fighting wore on, it was critical for both the Union and the Confederate forces that other nations allied with them or at least stayed neutral. Of particular concern was Great Britain, which, having lost the Revolutionary War against the US, many thought wanted to side with the Confederacy.

Knowing this, Lincoln dispatched Charles Francis Adams as the Ambassador to Great Britain, with a critical mission to at least to prevent Great Britain from joining forces with the Confederacy. Ideally, Adams could get them to support the Union or remain neutral.

Just as Benjamin Franklin was successful in convincing France to side with the US against Great Britain eighty years earlier, Adams now had to convince Great Britain to side with the Union and not join forces with the seceding Confederacy. His success or failure as the Ambassador would help determine the course of the war and the fate of the Union.

When you think of an *ambassador*, whom do you think of? Maybe Madeleine Albright, who served as the US Ambassador to the United Nations from 1993 to 1997, or perhaps Lynne Tracy or R. Nicholas Burns, who are the current US Ambassadors to Russia and China, respectively. While these great men and women represent the best interests of a nation on a global stage, there are many more who represent the best interests of smaller communities all around the world. They are the Ambassador archetype of Super Connectors.

The Ambassador is a Super Connector who excels at bringing two or more communities together toward a shared goal with their mutual interests in mind. The etymology of the word "ambassador" includes root words meaning "to be a servant," "of both sides," and "to guide," which are all apt descriptions of how Ambassadors work with communities. In doing so, Ambassadors amplify the impact of the communities they work with and serve the needs of a broader set of people. While other Super Connectors bring *individuals* together and work with a given community, Ambassadors bring *communities* together, working with multiple communities.

Ambassador Best Practices

In general, the Ambassador archetype of Super Connectors does the following things well to be effective in their roles:

1. They Understand the Communities Involved

They have to deeply understand not just the community they're from, but also the other community they are engaging with.

2. They Articulate a Common Shared Purpose

They have to be able to define why these communities are coming together and what greater purpose it serves.

3. They Articulate Mutual Value and Gain

They also have to be able to explain how the communities involved will benefit from the collaboration.

4. They Build Bridges Across the Communities

They connect people between the two communities to help act as the "bridges" between the communities.

5. They are Boundary-Spanning Leaders

More so than most other Super Connectors, they inhabit the space *between* the communities, being able to go back-and-forth between the communities, able to see both sides, take a neutral stance when needed, and so forth. They inhabit the *intersection* between communities.

6. They Bring a Certain Expertise

Whether it's climate change, cybersecurity, humanitarian needs, or something else that is relevant to the mission and to the communities involved, their specific expertise increases the trust that they know what they're doing.

7. They Understand Their Responsibility

They are charged with representing the best interests of multiple communities, and they view that as a responsibility not to be taken lightly.

Arno Michaelis

Let's take the case of Arno Michaelis. His is a fairly well-documented tale, with his own two books and many news articles about his amazing work. The following account is based on my conversations with him, along with what's already publicly available. As you read his story, please consider how he operated as an Ambassador by understanding the communities involved, articulating a clear mission and benefits, and what boundaries he crosses regularly to fulfill his mission.

Arno grew up in the suburbs of Milwaukee with two parents who loved him dearly and with adults around him who gave him plenty of positive affirmations and support. As he told it, even though they were not wealthy, he did not lack for anything materially. But there was a much darker side. Behind the scenes, there was a long history of alcoholism in his family that caused him a lot of emotional violence while growing up. He himself started drinking at age fourteen and from there went down an "ever-escalating path of bullying, physical violence, and eventually hate crimes."

In 1988, when he was just eighteen, he co-founded "what went on to become the largest white power skinhead organization on Earth." For the next several years, he went on an alcohol- and hate-fueled rampage of rage. He got into fights, beat people up to within inches of their lives, and almost died himself many times. He writes in his book, *My Life After Hate*:

> "In the absence of love's light, hate can be exciting, seductive. It beckons you and sends torrid, empty power coursing through your veins. At first, you think you can dabble. Just for kicks. Just a bit of entertainment to ripple the excruciating monotony of your disdain for the world. You blink, and you're covered in someone's blood. Another blink and the doors of your cell are slamming shut. A blink later and the image of your best friend's mannequin-looking corpse as cold and wooden and wrong as the open casket it sits in is seared into your brain forever. You rub your eyes in response to the blinks and the tears of your family run down your face. The tears of the parents of the people you battered beyond recognition. The tears of survivors who feel their children torn from their arms and their parents murdered all over again at the sight of you. That's how it happens... how it happened to me, at least."[4]

Then a couple of things happened that put him on a path of healing and out of hatred and violence.

First, his daughter was born when Arno was just twenty-two years old. Even through the haze of his rage and drunkenness, he knew upon meeting her that he loved her and also intuitively knew she would change his life. Then when she was just eighteen months old, her mother left them, and he became her sole guardian. At age twenty-four, he became a single dad. But unlike many other dads, he was a white-power skinhead racial warrior, his towering frame covered in tattoos, with a swastika on his middle finger for maximum hateful impact.

This is when the seeds of change started to take hold for him. He shared, "I called off the race war with the realization my daughter needed me. We were all each other had. Being a Racial Holy Warrior wasn't going to save my daughter; it would take me from her via death or prison. The more time I spent with her, the more it became imperative that I leave the movement."

At the same time, it began to really sink in for him how the people he was taught to hate—a Jewish boss, a lesbian supervisor, and black and Latino co-workers—when he spewed hatred and vitriol at them, they did not reply in kind, but instead replied with kindness. They "defied my hostility," he wrote. "They treated me with kindness when I least deserved it, but when I most needed it. These examples of how human beings should treat each other ultimately built upon an exhaustion that had me looking for an excuse to leave 'the movement.'"

Nearly two decades later, he is now an author, motivational speaker, filmmaker, and Ambassador for peace at Serve 2 Unite. He co-founded Serve 2 Unite in 2013 with Pardeep Kelaka, whose father tragically fell victim to a hate crime by a gunman who was a member of the white power skinhead gang Arno co-founded in the late 1980s. Together Arno and Pardeep formed this organization to work with young people from second grade through college to help them to "cherish diversity rather than fear it." They work "primarily with Milwaukee-based schools, bringing together students of all backgrounds to collaborate on art projects and activities, as well as participate in open discussions. Students are connected with Serve 2 Unite's global mentors, a network of peace activists who have either survived genocide, been involved in gangs, or previously promoted radical ideologies."

Arno is an Ambassador between two worlds: the communities of white supremacists he was a part of and the broader, more diverse society he has learned to embrace. More than perhaps most people, he deeply understands both worlds. Consider that not only did he live the life of a violent skinhead, but he co-founded and *recruited people* to create the largest hate group in America. He deeply understands the members' dark state of mind. He shared from his own experiences, "It's impossible to see how the hurt you emanate feels on the receiving end because you have no empathy for other humans." He also knows their doubts and fears because he experienced them himself. "I faintly recall whispers of don't do this... don't hurt them... coming from somewhere long ago in my soul." If anyone can reach them, he can.

He has clearly articulated a mission of peace and acceptance, and the benefits to the people involved are immense. Imagine what it means to get back your child, parent, sibling, or spouse who was lost in the world of hate, or what it means to know your children can grow up and live in a world that is more accepting of differences. He writes about an earlier time in his life as he was coming out of the hate community: "I arrived early to pick my daughter up from daycare. No one had noticed me, so I took in the moment, watching with teary eyes as my little girl played with the other kids. It struck me that the first thing I noticed was that they were all children, not black children or white children, but the sons and daughters of mothers and fathers." This is the kind of world he wants to help create.

He does not work alone. As an Ambassador, he builds bridges and makes connections across communities to fulfill that mission. He founded Serve 2 Unite *with* Pardeep to help heal the Sikh community that was so deeply affected by the hate crime in 2012. At Serve 2

Unite, "students are *connected with* Serve 2 Unite's global mentors," further empowering both the students and their mentors.

Some final words from Arno about why his work matters so much: "Because hurt people hurt people. Because when suffering isn't treated with compassion, it seethes and spreads. Because when fear isn't met with courage, it deceives and disconnects humans from humanity. When ignorance isn't countered with wisdom, it festers and takes root in the hearts of the fearful. When hatred isn't cradled with kindness, it can corrupt the beauty of existence to the extreme that causing suffering is the only thing that makes sense anymore. Rather than cultivate hatred with vengeance, we choose to commemorate our lost loved ones with the glory and grace of our common humanity. We choose to sow seeds of kindness and compassion."

Ambassadors, from Charles Francis Adams to Arno Michaelis, along with many others, have the power to change the world by bringing different communities together around a shared common good.

Next, let's consider an archetype related to Ambassadors in that they work across communities but are very different because they visit and inhabit multiple communities rather than bringing them together. Let's meet the Explorer.

Chapter 9 Notes

1. See https://avalon.law.yale.edu/19th_century/lincoln1.asp.
2. See https://www.cnn.com/2017/08/15/opinions/ex-white-power-compassion-answer-michaelis-opinion/index.html and https://www.cnn.com/2020/11/12/opinions/former-white-supremacist-how-to-tackle-hate-buckley/index.html.
3. See https://www.amazon.com/Life-After-Hate-Michaelis-Arno/dp/0983129096.

CHAPTER 10:
THE EXPLORER

"You are an explorer, and you represent our species, and the greatest good you can do is to bring back a new idea, because our world is endangered by the absence of good ideas."
~ Terrence McKenna ~

"Man cannot discover new oceans unless he has the courage to lose sight of the shore."
~ Andre Gide ~

Sir Robert Swan

Let's start with the story of Sir Robert Swan, OBE. Robert is a literal explorer. He is renowned as the first human to walk both the North and South Poles in 1989 and 1986, respectively. He has authored multiple books and is a sought-after motivational speaker. He also founded the 2041 Foundation, a nonprofit organization with the goal of saving Earth's polar regions. Their website states, "The mission of the 2041 Foundation is to engage businesses and communities on climate science, personal leadership, and the promotion of sustainable practices."[1] For these and his many other positive contributions to society, he was awarded the distinction of being an Officer of the Order of the British Empire (OBE).

Robert clearly explores distant lands. In January 2023, he completed another expedition to the South Pole with his son Barney and the South African documentary filmmaker Kyle O'Donoghue. What makes him a Super Connector Explorer isn't his traveling, though. Rather, it's more about how he "goes native" wherever he travels. He learns the locals' languages, eats their foods, and learns their customs. He takes the time to really get to know the people he meets during his voyages and thus forms meaningful, long-lasting relationships with people all around the world. This is what makes him a Super Connector Explorer. He explores not just places, but the peoples and communities in the places he travels to.

So far, we have met Super Connector archetypes that are somehow connected to specific communities. Superhosts create warm gatherings of people; Community Builders create communities that last over time; Catalysts move the community towards a shared purpose; Seers help the community to learn and make changes over time; Advocates promote individuals to help the community; Ambassadors connect one community with another, and so on. To be effective, they all work within one or more communities.

The Explorer is distinguished by the fact they are rarely found within a single community, at least not for long. Instead, they are usually found far afield in *other* communities, making new friends, learning new things, and discovering new ideas. They have a home base, and while Explorers need a safe and solid place to come home to, what they excel at is "being out there," meeting new people in different communities and making all kinds of fantastic discoveries.

Explorer Best Practices

Let's expand on this. The Explorer excels at the following things:

1. Crossing Boundaries

They travel to distant lands, meet different kinds of people, eat unusual foods, and hear new stories. Think about the late Anthony Bourdain, the celebrity chef, author, and travel documentarian with multiple shows, including the TV series *Parts Unknown,* where he traveled to different parts of the world and documented the local foods, flavors, and people. He said, "If I'm an advocate for anything, it's to move—as far as you can, as much as you can, across the ocean, or simply across a river. Walk in someone else's shoes or at least eat their food. It's a plus for everybody."[2]

In their travels, Explorers inevitably wind up crossing many kinds of boundaries—vast geographic distances, yes, but more to the point, dozens of languages and cultural differences, along with any prejudices and fears of the unknown. Explorers have developed an incredible ability to cross these boundaries and build rapport with "other" people very quickly.

2. Making New Discoveries/Bringing Back Treasures

More than any other Super Connector, the Explorer is the best at bringing new discoveries back to a community. Whether that's a new kind of food or spice, a new friend from a faraway land, a new idea or invention, or just the stories about their experiences, Explorers bring back unexpected but at times very useful resources to the home community.

3. Connecting the Dots

Explorers are the cousins of the Seers and are also able to connect the dots easily. Their special version of this power comes from their ability to see patterns across a vast array of different domains and experiences. They will see patterns others have missed because they often travel to and include perspectives from many different fields and communities.

4. High Trust/Courage

All Super Connectors are exceptional at building trust with other people and have a certain amount of self-confidence to be able to talk to and connect with all kinds of people. This is especially true for Explorers because they often find themselves in unfamiliar and, at times, very dangerous places. It takes a great deal of courage to brave such parts unknown at the risk of one's health and well-being to explore and meet new people. It's more than having a thick skin, it's knowing you can handle yourself in most, even dangerous, situations.

Now please keep that last point about courage in mind as we go back to the story of Sir Robert Swan to see what we mean.

Robert was born and raised in England. At the age of eleven, he was inspired after learning about the perilous journeys of Roald Amundsen and Robert Scott to the South Pole in 1912. He was absolutely fascinated by the South Pole, but it was Amudsen and Scott's stories of courage and determination that inspired him. He recalled thinking to himself at the time, "I want to, one day, walk to the north and south poles!"

His journey as an Explorer, and eventually to the Poles, began in 1974 when he was at Oxford University. He had been accepted on a sports scholarship to play rugby. He was rather good at it, he recalled, but said, "I didn't really like the idea of just being *given* something." So, in a rebellious and fateful moment, he decided to leave the University, leave England, leave his family and friends, and board a ship bound for Cape Town, South Africa. He was just eighteen years old at the time.

Now keep in mind that South Africa in the 1970s was a very tumultuous place, with the continuation and intensification of apartheid policies and significant resistance against apartheid from various groups resulting in social turmoil and violence. Cape Town, as a major port and economic hub for the country, was a bustling place, teeming with workers from all over the world. Working and living conditions for these migrant workers were poor and often dangerous. Once he got there he knew absolutely no one, and he didn't have money, so he needed a job.

He somehow managed to get a job driving a taxi around the docks at Cape Town. Now, many of his customers turned out to be "ladies of the night" whom he would shuttle from one docked ship to another so they could rendezvous with their sailor clients from all around the world. He recalled, "This was South Africa in the middle of Apartheid, and the docks were a dangerous place with a lot of violence. And there I was, this dumb eighteen-year-old white kid from England driving taxis around to make some money. I was so young and naive!"

Fortunately for him, these ladies decided to take him under their wing. "I remember them all so clearly!" he said. "They were extraordinary women" from different backgrounds and nationalities, blacks, Indians and others, people whom he had, until then, never really had an opportunity to speak with. They taught him how to stay safe, what areas to avoid, and generally how to survive. As he put it, "They looked after me, and gave me all the best jobs."

He, in turn, looked after them, and gradually, they became friends, and this resulted in a very important lesson for him. He said, "What these ladies of the night did for me is that my friendship with them broke this barrier where I, as this white, privileged young man, really understood that I could be exactly as I was and that there was no difference between myself and them. I knew that someone in a position of privilege and education could look down on certain other people because they're prostitutes or something else. But being with these ladies broke this barrier for me of color, race, creed, and education. So that was a big deal for me as a kid, and I've taken that lesson of crossing barriers through the rest of my life."

When asked why he thinks they took him under their wing, he reflected and shared, "I think because I wasn't jaded, and that I was rather 'English polite.' That's how I was educated and raised, to be courteous. For example, I would open the door for them as their taxi driver, not because I was trying to impress them, but because that was the way I was brought up. I would go the extra step to be helpful." He added, "And also that I truly wanted to understand them. I would ask them questions: 'Where are you from?', or 'How does this work?' And I think they saw the authenticity, genuineness, and curiosity of this young, eighteen-year-old kid."

By now, I'm sure you recognize the core common traits of Super Connectors, such as being curious and being a giver. His curiosity about these ladies led him to really get to know them as people and build genuine friendships with them based on deep trust. His giving nature, his natural instinct to go the extra mile to be helpful also endeared him to them. Their friendship, along with their patronage, enabled him to survive the dangerous streets of Cape Town and earn a living.

After a while, he was able to save enough money from his work to go on his next big adventure, which was a trek from Cape Town to Cairo – on a bicycle! Have you ever mapped a path from Cape Town to Cairo? The shortest path available on Google Maps today is 9,697 km (6,025 miles) by car, cutting through Botswana, Zambia, Tanzania, Uganda, South Sudan, and finally Sudan before reaching Cairo. Google Maps does not even offer an option to make this trek on a bicycle! Keep in mind, he did this in the 1970s, before PCs, the Internet, and mobile phones.

He planned for this to be a seven-month journey, but things didn't go according to plan, and as you might imagine, he encountered many difficulties along the way, some quite life-threatening. An illustrative story takes place towards the end of his journey. As he told it, "I got to Sudan after about six and a half months on a bicycle. And I got to this village, Atbara, which was on the edge of the Nubian Desert, some 300-odd miles south of Egypt." He arrived at the train station in Atbara and figured he would bike across the desert to Egypt by following the train tracks.

Unfortunately, he had by then contracted trypanosomiasis, also known as African sleep sickness, caused by infected tse tse flies, which "makes you want to sleep for 18–20 hours a day." He set out on his bicycle, had a really bad day of it, and turned around. Back at the station, when he asked when the next train to Egypt would be, he was told it would be a week. Given the disease and his fatigue, he simply found a quiet spot at the station, propped up his bike against a wall, and went to sleep next to it, thinking he just might die there.

In the middle of the night, he was woken up by a man who told Robert he could not stay in the station. Upon learning of Robert's journey and illness, he invited Robert to his home to rest until the train arrived in a week. The kind man's name was Mohammed, and he was a local school teacher. He opened up his home, and he offered to look after Robert and help him recuperate. In return, he asked Robert to speak with him and his family in English, so they could practice the language. Robert gratefully agreed.

At Mohammed's home, Mohammed and his family sheltered Robert in a room, brought him food, gave him medicine, and nursed him back to health. During Robert's waking moments, they would sit with him, sharing stories, practicing English, and learning about each other. Until then, he had not spent any time in a Muslim household. Robert had "no concept at all about the Muslim religion" and no idea it was Ramadan at the time, the holiest month of the year for Muslims. Crossing over to Mohammed's world and spending time with his family was another completely new experience for him, meeting people who were different from him, as he had done with the ladies at the docks in Cape Town.

After a week, much recovered from his illness, well-fed, and better rested, he found himself back at the train station, bidding farewell to Mohammed and his family. From there, he completed his trek to Cairo via train and then made his way back to England, back to his family and friends, and back to Oxford University. But this lesson of "crossing over" into other countries and cultures and connecting with people who are very different from him (at least on the surface) stayed with him. He reflected, "Now when I see stories of the bad side of Islam and people killing each other, blowing each other up and all that, I always have this beautiful vision in my mind about Mohammed's family." He deeply internalized the insight that despite all our perceived external differences, on the inside we're all the same, all human, and "brother, not other" with each other.

This lesson in humanity was critical to his success as an Arctic explorer. Let's fast forward about twenty years to his next story.

In 1986, after he and his team successfully completed their trek to the South Pole, he set his sights on the North Pole. Now, one might think that the North And South Poles are the same – cold, icy places. But unlike the South Pole, he knew that to make it to the North Pole, they would be going across a frozen ocean, about 700 miles of it! Since the North Pole is actually located in the middle of the Arctic Ocean, covered by shifting sea ice, he and his team would have to trek over a surface that is constantly shifting and breaking up, around various hazards such as open waters, ice piles, thin ice that you could fall through, and so on. The trouble was that no one in his team knew how to do this!

But Robert knew the Soviet Union had some of the world's best experts in crossing the Arctic Ocean. There was one man in particular, Dr. Mikhail Malakhov, whom he knew had done a number of expeditions, and was "bloody good, the best." Plus, he was a medical doctor, which would be really helpful on a dangerous mission like this. Robert wanted to recruit Dr. Malakhov, but they didn't know each other. Furthermore, "It was put into our heads that the Soviets were the enemy." He remembered how as a kid, they had "duck and cover exercises" at school to prepare for a possible bombing from the Soviets and that "every film and everything that you watched, it was all saying that the Soviets are our mortal enemy."

Undaunted, Robert flew to the Soviet Union, went to the town where he knew Dr. Malakhov lived, and found him. Robert then did two things that earned Dr. Malakhov's trust and got him to agree to join the expedition.

First, Robert took the time to get to know Dr. Malakhov, his family, and his life. He recalled, "He was just this unbelievable fellow. I went to his local town, met with him and his family, and got to know him really well." Just as he had done many times before in other parts of the world, he was able to connect with Dr. Malakhov as a human being, beyond all the social constructs that marked him as an "other" and an "enemy."

For the second part, he had to earn Dr. Malakhov's trust. Robert explained: "I think trust is a very important part of any exploration. And the thing with trust is, if you don't trust yourself, how the hell is anybody ever going to trust you? A lot of people talk about trusting other people, but it doesn't count if you don't trust yourself."

To him, this meant knowing what he was capable of and what he was not good at, and being very honest with others about both. About Dr. Malakhov (whom he now affectionately calls "Misha") he said, "A Soviet doctor doesn't want some big podcast about how great you are. Instead, I told him, 'Look, by some miracle, I managed to make it to the South Pole,' so he knows I can do it. But I also told him, 'I know nothing about going across the Arctic Ocean. I can put the expedition together, I can raise the money, but when it comes to actually executing the final journey, I can't do that, and I need you to please take that on.'"

This is where he extended his trust to Misha. He told Misha, "I'll get everybody to the starting line. But once we start, you're in charge. And I'm not going to look over your shoulder. Whatever you decide, we as a team will follow because you're in charge." He explained, "I think you gain huge trust with people by really trusting them. And I think that when he looked at me, he realized I was for real." Robert had earned Misha's trust, and he agreed to join Robert's mission to the North Pole.

The team Robert assembled was called Icewalkers, made up of eight people from seven nations. As part of their trek, the team carried out a range of scientific tests and experiments related to the Arctic's environmental conditions and the impact of climate change and pollution in the area and on our planet.

They successfully completed their mission on May 14, 1989. A few days later, after returning to London, they met with the Prime Minister at the time, Margaret Thatcher. The United Press International quoted Robert as saying, "We've opened a line of communication with a Prime Minister who we believe is making a genuine effort to do something about the survival of this planet, and that's what we're talking about" after he met with Thatcher at her Downing Street residence."[3]

His mission expanded from there to fighting the effects of climate change for humanity. According to Wikipedia, "In 1992, Swan was invited by the United Nations to be a keynote speaker at the first Earth

Summit for Sustainable Development in Rio de Janeiro, Brazil. In response to the world leaders' challenge to "think global, act local," Swan made a commitment to deliver a global and local environmental mission involving industry, business, and young people to the next World Summit in 2002."

To this day, Misha remains a close family friend of Robert. He is the Godfather to Robert's son, Barney, for example. Misha came to visit Robert and his family in the US some twenty-five years ago. Robert's mother was eighty years old at the time and had been taking pills to treat the symptoms of some of her ailments. Misha looked at the drugs and said, "Mr. Swan, I'm going to take these and throw them away." He treated her using more natural remedies he was aware of, and as of the time of my interview with him, she was 106 years old and still going strong!

Let's review some key aspects from Robert's stories that make him an Explorer type of Super Connector:

Crossing Boundaries: As an explorer, Robert clearly crosses many difficult physical and geographic boundaries, but as a Super Connector Explorer, he crosses many challenging social boundaries. He did so with the ladies in South Africa, Mohammed and his family in Sudan, Misha from Russia, and many others. He connects with people genuinely as friends and family—brother, sister, aunt, uncle— and not as an "other."

Making New Discoveries/Bringing Back Treasures: Robert was able to recruit Misha because he was able to cross the boundary to the Soviet Union, cross the cultural divide and mistrust, and bring back a lifelong friend. From his time in South Africa, Sudan, and other places, he was able to learn about other peoples and cultures, bringing back not just great memories but also timeless lessons about our shared humanity.

Connecting the Dots: Because of their many travels to distant lands and peoples, Super Connector Explorers are able to connect the dots across many different domains and see the big picture. Robert's personal travels to both poles give him a unique perch and perspective from which to advocate for helping make the world more sustainable. He noted, for example, how the younger generations now are "angry with us" for making the world the way it is now and observed that "this planet is going to look after itself. It's our survival on it that's in question."

High Trust/Courage: Explorers cannot do what they do without a deep sense of trust in themselves, the knowledge they can handle most situations, and the courage to brave the unknown. He reminds us, however, that this is a journey. "What you have to do to truly trust yourself is to understand that it's always and forever a work in progress." As we have to do it with others, we have to continue to earn and build our trust in ourselves.

Beth Dochnger

Let's now consider another example, one closer to home. With this story, I want to show that one does not have to endure physically challenging conditions in faraway places (such as the North Pole, the depths of the ocean, or outer space) to be an Explorer.

Beth Dochnger was just six years old when she got on an airplane for the first time. What's remarkable about this event is that she went on the plane by herself, without her family. Every summer from the time she was six, she would travel by airplane from Ohio, where she lived with her family, to visit her grandparents in New York City. She recalled, "I was not afraid. I was going to go see my grandparents!"

Her grandfather was a loving figure in her life who always encouraged her to explore and make new friends. She has wonderful memories of walking around in New York City with him "for miles and miles." He used these occasions to teach her to be independent, think on her own, and connect with people who were different from her. Thanks partially to his encouragement, she learned to make many friends on these flights between Ohio and New York City. She shared, "My mother would put me on an airplane all by myself. I would sit near the stewardesses, and I even got to serve coffee on occasion to the other passengers on these flights. I made friends with everyone, including the captains, stewardesses, and other passengers. It was TWA, and I still have my junior stewardess wings!"

She grew up in a small family of four, where her parents were both only children, and she had only one sibling. Theirs was also a Jewish household, and she noticed how there were not a lot of other Jewish families. As a result, she had to make an effort to connect with other families and make friends in different circles. For example, she remembers a group of women who played Mahjong with her mother, and they became family, her "aunts." She has great memories of being a Girl Scout, camping, learning survival activities, learning how to be more independent, and doing things without adult supervision at an early age.

One of the most impactful aspects of her life was music. As she grew up, she played with the local community orchestra and attended summer camps at the prestigious Interlochen Center for the Arts in Michigan where she held fourth chair in the World Youth Orchestra. Later, she studied flute performance at University of Michigan. While she did not stay in music as her career, she is still lifelong friends with her classmates, many of whom went on to become famous and accomplished musicians.

Instead, her passion for music, combined with her passion for traveling and meeting new people, led her to a career in fundraising and development for non-profit organizations. This happened when she was studying at the University of Cincinnati for her master's degree in Arts Administration. Her advisor thought she would be great in development, and he and his wife, the Dean of the music school, encouraged her to pursue this path after completing her master's.

Eventually, this led Beth to a career in development and fundraising for the arts. She excelled at it and thrived, both personally and professionally, because it also fed her love for exploration and meeting new people. At one point in her career, she drove between 300 and 600 miles in three days, meeting 8–10 people during that time. "My job was to go and visit people who had never been visited before to assess their willingness to make a major gift." She traveled all over the United States and Canada, totaling 100–250 visits each year, along with countless miles!

Outside of work, she was still drawn to meet and understand all kinds of people, so in her free time (to "test myself," she adds), she traveled to exotic places, and met with the locals. For example, one year she bicycled around the Ring of Kerry, the beautiful 111-mile circular route in County Kerry in southwestern Ireland. She stayed at local venues and castles, meeting and interacting with lots of locals along the way.

She has also ridden with a Harley Davidson bike gang from Toledo, Ohio. She recalled fondly how they used to call her the "Porcelain Princess." She also sailed and worked on the *Adventure* (an apt name), the last of the great windjammers, which were large sailing ships that were used primarily in the late 19th and early 20th centuries for transporting cargo.

Ireland, a Harley Davidson gang, and a sailboat from the early 1900s? Talk about different worlds! But from these and many of her other travels, she shared this about the various people she had met: "These were people who were no different than me. They worked and lived their lives with their families." She is making the same observation that Robert has made about our shared humanity, no matter our outward differences. Maybe more than most other Super Connector archetypes, the Explorer has the opportunity to really notice this in their travels.

Let's consider some of Beth's best practices and how they match up with Robert's:

Crossing Boundaries: Beth, too, clearly crosses social boundaries. Robert made friends with a Muslim and a Russian; Beth made friends with a Harley Davidson bike gang and potential donors. She regularly crosses the threshold of people's lives and connects with them meaningfully, both for her work and for personal adventure. She seeks and finds kinship with whomever she meets.

Making New Discoveries/Bringing Back Treasures: She literally brings back a bounty of treasures in the form of funds for the nonprofits she supports, but also brings back amazing experiences, memories, keepsakes, and friendships.

Connecting the Dots: Beth has developed a deep understanding of what people want through the thousands of visits she's had with potential donors. Regardless of where they live and where they are in their lives, she understands their motivations and how they align with the desire to donate and contribute to a cause.

High Trust/Courage: She noted that especially as a woman traveling to places unknown and meeting new people, she has to be careful and, more importantly, she has to have high trust in herself, that she knows how to take care of herself. She uses her exceptionally high emotional intelligence to assess situations and the people she meets, connect meaningfully, build rapport, and go from there.

Because the Explorer is often "out there" traveling, it can be difficult to find them. You usually have to wait for them to return home to connect with them. In the next chapter, we'll meet a Super Connector who is also relatively difficult to find but, unlike the Explorer, is usually rooted in one community: The Elder.

Chapter 10 Notes

1. See https://2041foundation.org/about-us.
2. See https://www.inc.com/justin-bariso/this-beautiful-anthony-bourdain-quote-is-a-masterpiece-of-emotional-intelligence.html.
3. See http://bufvc.ac.uk/tvandradio/lbc/index.php/segment/0005300365006.

CHAPTER 11:
THE ELDER

"The role of culture is that it's the form through which we as a society reflect on who we are, where we've been, where we hope to be."
~ Wendell Pierce ~

Shiva Sapkota

Shiva Sapkota spent the first sixteen years of his life growing up in a refugee camp in Nepal.

The United Nations describes refugee camps as "temporary facilities built to provide immediate protection and assistance to people who have been forced to flee their homes due to war, persecution or violence."[1] That does not begin to describe what it's really like.

Shiva described to me an environment that "lacks all types of resources: technology, electricity, basic necessities like clean drinking water. There were no medical facilities and no schools." Death was an everyday occurrence. He recalled, "You know, we used to just drink water straight from the river. Malaria was rampant. Cobras are very common over there, and because there were no hospitals to treat you, people were dying all the time."

Even if you escaped death, life was a miserable experience. Hunger was an everyday experience. Because their "homes were made with bamboo and plastic coverings, every time it rained, there would be a leak." They also had no beds, so everyone slept on the floor.

This is where he was born, as the youngest of six children. His family is *Lhotshampa*, which means they are Bhutanese people of Nepalese descent. Starting in the 1980s, the Bhutanese government instituted a series of practices to strip the Lhotshampa of their Bhutan citizenship and expel them from their country. Many, hundreds of thousands of them actually, wound up in this refugee camp in Nepal. It was a traumatic experience, to say the least, and even at his current age of thirty, Shiva still has nightmares of that time.

For years, the United Nations worked to relocate these refugees from the refugee camp to other countries where they could immigrate and start new lives. In 2008, when Shiva was sixteen, he and his family were moved out of the camp to Aurora, Colorado. To say the change was a culture shock is an understatement, and to make matters worse, because they were among the first Bhutanese refugees there, they knew no one. "We didn't know anyone, and we didn't know how to do anything," Shiva recalled. "We were just put in an apartment, and for two days we didn't even eat because we didn't know how to use the rice cooker or the stove or any of that." They had to learn how to cook using appliances they'd never seen, how to use the bus to get around, where to get groceries, how to apply to go to school, how to apply for jobs, and so forth.

When Shiva attended high school later that year, he struggled with not knowing English, learning how to navigate through the school system and the sadly predictable teasing and bullying that ensued. He shared this story about his first day at school: "So I walked in, and nobody looks like me and nobody tells me anything. I go in, they give me my schedule, and I get to my first class. And, you know, in Nepal, you're supposed to say, 'May I come in?' before you walk into the class. So I stand in front of the classroom and I said, 'May I come in?' in Nepalese, and everybody just started laughing. So it was that kind of a shock every single day as I learned how to go to school."

There were two things that sustained him and his family as they made their way in Aurora: gratitude and perseverance. They were grateful for being alive and for being given this chance at a new life. They also had an attitude of perseverance, that "tomorrow is going to be better than today," and that today they would do everything they could to make things better. This is exactly what they had to do to survive in the refugee camp in Nepal. Surely Aurora could not be worse!

In school, Shiva was determined to learn everything he could. For example, he would get up very early in the morning and go to the library to study. There he came across a computer for the first time in his life and learned how to use it. "I stayed up after school, talking to my teachers, talking to anyone I could find to help me to learn."

As for English, he shared, "Believe it or not, I joined the speech and debate team to learn English. In the beginning, people laughed at me because I'm up there with my broken English," but he persevered, and by the time he graduated from high school, he had competed in national debate championships, participated in various mock trials, and had gotten to meet many lawyers and judges from around the country. In fact, he graduated in the *top ten* of his high school, and he was offered multiple scholarships to attend various universities. "It wasn't easy," he recalled, "but at the end of the day, you know, I look back at that time, and I'm really glad I didn't give up and kept pushing forward."

Another thing that sustained him and his family was community. At the refugee camp in Nepal, despite the many daily challenges—or maybe more accurately, because of them—there was a very strong sense of community, and everyone came together to help each other. For example, when a fire broke out in the camp, it would spread quickly, especially during the windy season, and "wipe out the entire camp." Everyone would have to move into the forest to shelter and live there for a while, and the community would come together to help rebuild everyone's homes. They would share what meager food and resources they had to help everyone to survive. "I think this is what kept us alive in the camp: that everybody was super helpful in the community," he reflected. "What we had was everybody coming together and saying, 'We're gonna do this, and we're going to do this together.'"

He brought this same mentality to the community of Bhutanese refugees in Aurora, which was very small at the time. "I realized I didn't want anybody else to go through the same experience I had. So what I started doing was helping other refugee families before school, after school, and on weekends." He would go to their homes and help them fill out forms with the Health Care Center, where they took in refugees and could apply for Medicaid. He would go to the airport and wait for a new refugee family to arrive "because whenever they come out of that plane, I wanted to make sure they had a familiar face they can talk to, speak in the language they know, and have an experience of knowing they are not alone here, that there are other people like them here." He would then drive them to their apartments and show them how to use the stove for cooking, where to go for food stamps, where to get groceries, how to take the bus, and so on.

What happened then, slowly but surely, was that the families he helped wanted to do what he did for them and help other refugees. So he taught them "how you do things, how you make an impact." As more of his friends helped other immigrants and their impact increased, they built up their confidence and eventually realized, "Okay, we can do this!" And then something magical happened. "It just became a community, like the community we had back in the camp. It kind of replicated itself here in the United States."

In the same way that everybody came together to help each other at the refugee camp in Nepal, everybody was there to help each other in Aurora, CO. For example, if someone in the community passed away, everyone in the community would show up for the funeral. In fact, the people who worked at the funeral homes noticed how their parking lots were full whenever there was a death in the Nepalese community. The same thing would happen at happy occasions such as weddings, graduations, birthdays, and so forth. Everybody would show up for one another. "And that is the passion I have with the community, and the community itself is so passionate about helping each other."

Over time, this community became national, spreading to all fifty States, as many of the immigrants in Aurora moved to other states and as other Bhutanese refugees arrived into those other states. Shiva's network of helpers, as they also moved out to other cities and states, helped other immigrants in those locations. The Bhutanese refugee community in the US is now about 100,000. To put that in context, Aurora has 300,000 residents, so Shiva noted how his community nationally is about the size of a large town. He's strongly connected to many of them around the country. "I can go to any state and have a place to stay, have food to eat, and go be with people because of how connected the community was during those times."

Let's pause here to consider this more deeply. Through Shiva's years of dedicated service to other Bhutanese refugees in the US, the community has thrived and grown to number about 100,000 people around the country. He may not know all of them, but most of them know who he is and what he has done for them. As a result, everywhere he goes, he has grateful friends who will welcome him into their homes.

Please note that Shiva has no official position of power here. He is not the official leader of this community of 100,000 refugees, nor is he their representative. He is not the CEO of a nonprofit that helps these refugees (he had started one years ago but handed the reins over to others after a while). In fact, his day job is to work as a mechanical engineer for the City of Aurora.

At the ripe old age of thirty-two, he is what I call an *Elder*.

Being an Elder is not about their age nor their official role in the community. It's much more about the standing they have within the community as someone who everyone else looks up to as the standard bearer and culture keeper of the community. Through their words and their actions, Elders demonstrate and reinforce the values and standards of the community, all of which help the community to thrive.

Here are some of the best practices for being an Elder that Shiva demonstrates:

1. Be Helpful

For Shiva, it was about wanting to help other refugee families as they made their way to Aurora. He showed up for them personally, and connected them to each other and to other people who could help them, such as aid workers, DMV personnel, and so on. He still helps them as best he can.

2. Espouse Community Values

The values of Shiva's community include having each other's backs and having solidarity as a community. Culturally, there is no sense of "I'm better than you because I've done well and made a lot of money." Instead, there is a desire to support the community that was so helpful to them when they were struggling and trying to make it in the past.

For example, when some members do well professionally, they would often come to Shiva asking for his input on how they can best contribute, whether by sponsoring a soccer tournament, buying laptops for students, or helping build a temple. As the community members help one another like this, the community continues to stay together and thrive.

Of course, we again see many of the core common traits of all Super Connectors. Clearly, he is a *giver* who gave of himself tirelessly to help other refugee families. He has earned the *trust* of hundreds of thousands of people, not just the families he has helped, but also others involved in the process as well, including his teachers, workers at the immigration office, TSA officials at the airport, people at the DMV, and so forth. He is also clearly *community-minded* and *purpose-driven* in his efforts.

3. Be Present

Ultimately, though, it's about helping to maintain the culture and values of the community, and to do that, you have to be present. The Elder cannot help uphold the values and norms of the community if he or she is not fully present and actively engaged with the community. Shiva showed up in person, in the mornings, evenings, and weekends to help his fellow refugees. He is still very actively engaged with the community.

That said, Elders usually do not seek the limelight for themselves. They often don't hold official positions of power, so they can be hard to spot unless you know where to look for them. And in the case of the next example of the Elder, you can usually find him on the dance floor!

Carlito Rofoli

West Coast Swing (WCS), known as the "official dance of California," was started by a swing dancer named Dean Collins. He moved from New York to California in 1936 and began to win contests with his own style of swing dancing. He and his dance partner, Jewel McGowen, got movie roles in the 1940s, further popularizing their unique style. The dance evolved over the years but maintained its distinctive smooth style, emphasizing partner connection and improvisation. It's versatile, and WCS dancers can groove to all kinds of music, from Big Band Swing to Jazz, R&B, Funk, Disco, Pop, Hip-hop, and many others.

Fast forward to 2023, and the dance has spread worldwide, with hundreds of thousands of avid fans attending WCS dance conventions to compete and learn from one another. The community actively welcomes beginners, and at some dance conventions, dancers are awarded prizes for being extra social and dancing with as many newcomers as possible. Dance lessons often include dance etiquette, again emphasizing the friendly and inclusive nature of this growing community.

Now, if you were to attend enough of these WCS dance conventions, you might notice there is often a director's chair reserved for one man in particular: Carlito Rofoli. The chair has his name on one side and the words "The Beginner" on the other side. Carlito is not a champion-level competitive dancer nor an official judge of competitions (though he used to be both in years past). Nor is he the leader of any group that organizes and runs these events. According to him, he is "just a street dancer from Hawaii."

So how does this eighty-eight-year-old genial man from Hawaii get his own named chair reserved for him at various West Coast Swing dance conventions? No other dancer, not even the champions or judges, get their own named chairs. Let's see how he exemplifies the role of an Elder in this community without even knowing he was doing so!

Carlito was born in Hawaii in 1935 to Filipino parents who sadly passed away around the time of the Pearl Harbor bombing during World War II. His eldest sister worked hard to raise him and his six other siblings.

It was a difficult childhood, but Carlito has always had a positive attitude. One of the ways in which he stayed positive was through dancing. "I had a bug as a dancer as a little boy," he recalled. "Filipino ancestry, always music and dancing in my family!" He and his extended family loved to dance, and he remembered dancing with his sisters and aunts at family gatherings while growing up.

He moved to California in 1965, and he picked up West Coast Swing soon after that. He couldn't afford private lessons, so he attended as many group workshops as possible, observed other dancers, asked many questions, and competed whenever possible. He eventually became a champion-level West Coast Swing dancer and taught for many years before retiring.

None of that, however, explains how he got his own chair at dance conventions. There are hundreds of thousands of other avid dancers in the community, along with hundreds of teachers and champions.

This part of the story takes place in 2015 when he had his first opportunity to travel internationally for West Coast Swing. The dance organizers in Budapest invited him to attend their annual convention. When his friends suggested they go, he answered with his customary cheerfulness, "Why not?"

When he arrived at the dance convention in Budapest (the event is called "Budafest"), he was surprised to find the woman who checked him in knew who he was.

"Hi, I'm Carlito," he said.

"Hi Carlito! Yes, we know who you are, welcome!" she answered.

Confused, he asked, "How do you know who I am? This is my first time in Europe. I don't know any of the dancers. I know the teachers who flew in here from the US, but that's all."

She smiled and said, "You may not know the people in Europe, but trust me, they know who you are. You have a fan club here!"

She then ushered him to meet with the event organizers, who paused in the middle of their busy schedule preparing for the convention to speak with him. They welcomed him to Budapest and asked how his trip was. After a bit of friendly conversation, they showed him his chair. "Carlito, The Beginner," it read.

Moved and quite perplexed, he asked them why they had done this. They explained, "Before we had our own WCS events in Europe, we would go to the US to learn how to dance. Every dance convention we went to in different States, you were there! And every time one of our ladies danced with you, they would tell the other girls, beaming, 'You gotta dance with him!'"

To say that his dance reputation precedes him would be an understatement! So what did he do that made all the girls want to dance with him so much that he developed a fan base in Europe?

He said his secret is how he lets the women "dance their dance." He doesn't try to go for fancy steps but instead provides the "frame" for them to express themselves and have a good time. "When I dance, it's not for me; it's for my followers," he explained. He usually sticks to the basic steps, with variations to provide an "illusion" of complexity, but focuses on making sure the follower looks great and has a great time.

He said he learned all this by observing others and asking questions. "Everything I've learned, I've learned from someone else." In high school, he asked the girls what they did not like about dancing with others so he could avoid doing that himself "so that women don't mind dancing with me!" Ever the "Beginner," wherever he went, he asked questions and sought to learn. Even now, he has a beginner's mind and seeks to learn. He can be found saying, "You have to pardon my ignorance. Compared to your education, I'm way behind!"

He's also one of the friendliest dancers you'll meet. He often wears a tee shirt with a smiley face that matches the genuine smile on his face. He told me his attitude is to love and be positive. "What choice do I have?" he asked. He will easily strike up a conversation with someone who seems lost at a dance convention or gently lead a beginner through a song or two on the dance floor. He makes everyone feel welcome and happier from having met him.

What makes Carlito an Elder in the West Coast Swing dance community is not his age, which he wears with his big smile and customary grace. It's how he exemplifies the values and norms of the community, so much so that he helped extend the community into Europe! He focuses on helping his followers have a wonderful time, which then helps spread the love of the dance to other followers as well as to other leaders who want to have the same positive effect on their followers. He is friendly and welcoming to everyone, which helps newcomers feel less intimidated and more at home. He's also constantly curious and learning, an essential trait for dancers to hone their skills and improve. These are the norms and values of the West Coast Swing dance community.

Of course, he's been a fixture of the community for decades. He learned the dance alongside other living legends such as Kelly Casanova, who still works as the Chief Judge at many WCS dance conventions. During that time, he visited many communities, attended many dance events, and developed long-lasting friendships with many other dancers all around the country. In other words, he's been an active community member as a teacher, champion, judge, and friend to many for decades. He developed thousands of relationships (including his many fans in Europe), enabling him to positively impact the community as one of its Elders.

Carlito is not the only Elder in the West Coast Swing dance community, though he is the only one, so far, with his own chair! But collectively, these standard bearers earn their community members' love and trust and help to strengthen their community by upholding the values and norms that make that community thrive.

We next conclude our overview of the eleven Archetypes with The Sage. While the words "Elder" and "Sage" might have similar images of a sagacious village elder, you'll see that the Sage archetype is quite different from the Elder.

Chapter 11 Notes

1.   See https://www.unrefugees.org/refugee-facts/camps.

CHAPTER 12:
THE SAGE

"Mastery, I learned, was not something genetic, or for a lucky few. It is something we can all attain if we get rid of some misconceptions and gain clarity as to the required path."
~ Robert Greene
(author of six international best sellers including Mastery) ~

The popular television animation series on Nickelodeon called *Avatar, the Last Air Bender* takes place in a world where its people can control, or "bend," one of the four elements of nature: air, water, earth, and fire. The series tells the story of Ang, the Avatar, who alone can master all four elements and must fight the evil Firelord, who is intent on taking over the world with his fiery powers. In the final epic battle, Ang is able to wield all four elements interchangeably and at will—for example, creating a force field made up of all four elements to surround and protect him, or launching a dizzying array of attacks using the various elements—to subdue and defeat the Firelord.

During my more than 150 interviews with Super Connectors, I've found they often inhabit more than one archetype. For example, a Superhost is also often a Matchmaker, inviting people to dinner parties and deftly making connections among the guests. Or an Explorer might also be a Seer who can synthesize new insights from very diverse and unexpected sources of information. In other words, while most Super Connectors have a preferred way of being (their primary archetype), they often have practices belonging to other archetypes.

Occasionally, I would meet a Super Connector who is masterful at being *several* archetypes at once. Like Avatar Ang with control over multiple elements, these Super Connectors have mastery over numerous archetypes, and can easily deploy various Super Connector skills as needed.

I call this kind of Super Connector a *Sage*. A 'sage' is a person who is regarded as having profound wisdom, knowledge, and experience. In the context of this book, the Sage is someone who is adept at being multiple archetypes of Super Connectors as needed and has the wisdom and experience to know which to be in a given situation.

For example, when I first met Barry Palte, I thought he might be an Ambassador or an Explorer. It quickly became apparent in our interviews he is also a Seer, a Catalyst, and possibly others. Let's consider his story to see how he does this.

Barry Palte

Like many other Super Connectors we've read about, Barry currently lives a life spanning multiple worlds. Barry is currently the Chairman of EQ Capital Partners in Sydney, Australia. EQ Capital Partners is a private firm that invests in companies that have social and environmental impact. He is also the Chairperson at Impact Rooms, a leading African investment platform that connects entrepreneurs, innovation, and capital at scale, based in Nairobi, Kenya. He is on the advisory board for MustGrow Biologics, a publicly traded agriculture biotech company focused on providing natural science-based biological solutions for high-value crops, based in Saskatchewan, Canada. He is also the Chief Investment Officer at Contour Companies, a fully vertically integrated real estate group based in Bloomfield Hills, Michigan, focused on restoring and uplifting communities. He speaks multiple languages and often travels the world for one cause or another (think Explorer or Catalyst).

He grew up inhabiting multiple worlds as well. He is Jewish by heritage but was born and raised in Zimbabwe as the son of a very wealthy family. His family owned one of the largest food manufacturing companies on the continent, and they lived in a large mansion with many servants. When civil war broke out in Zimbabwe (The Rhodesian Bush War, 1964–1979), conditions became too dangerous for them to continue living there, so Barry's father decided to move the whole family out of Zimbabwe, leaving everything behind.

They fled to South Africa, where Apartheid was in effect (1948–1994). Barry remembered, "It was like going from the frying pan to the fire" regarding social and political unrest. He was just fifteen at the time and did not understand why Apartheid was in place. In Zimbabwe, he had grown up seeing no differences based on race. He recalls having two loving mother figures in his life: one was his biological mother, who is white, and the other was his African nanny, who helped raise him as her own. Because of this loving upbringing, he was deeply disturbed by what he saw in South Africa. He vowed that when he grew up, he would work to "build bridges" between people. "This is fundamentally what drives me," he told me, "building bridges between as many cultures, languages, religions, skin colors, whatever it might be in the world" (think Ambassador).

Let's pause here to make a couple of observations about Barry's upbringing.

As with many other Super Connectors, Barry has lived a boundary-spanning life. He was a young white Jewish boy living in a mixed-race household in Zimbabwe. When they fled to South Africa, they were effectively refugees for a while, unable to renew their visas from Zimbabwe nor get new ones from South Africa. This boundary-crossing dislocation and "seeing things from another side" is a common early experience for Super Connectors.

Due to that experience, Barry experienced a strong desire to connect with people and belong. Recall how when Ryan Groves (Chapter 5) attended college, he felt alone, so he created a community of friends around him called the "Breakfast Bowtie Club" who held events to support a worthy cause. When Arabella Delucca (Chapter 8) immigrated to America, she felt different from her peers, so she created a greater sense of belonging for other minorities by advocating for them. Barry decided he wanted to build bridges between people.

Let's get back to his story to see how he did it.

Barry was gifted with natural intelligence and was able to attend the best university in South Africa on a full scholarship. After university, he moved to Australia to start his career in finance. His intellect, combined with his innate curiosity about people and his ability to connect the dots, enabled him to be very successful. He quickly rose through the ranks and held leadership roles at various financial services companies. He specialized in international business, including with China, where he did business for more than twenty years by building deep, trusted relationships with various leaders in the Chinese government and corporations.

Barry the Ambassador

When I asked him how a Jewish man from Australia who does *not* speak Chinese could be so successful working in China, he chuckled and said, "I pay attention to what matters, I respect the culture, and I become a part of their family."

He recounted a particularly telling story. He was invited to have lunch in China with an Australian friend who was working in China at the time as the Chairman of an international bank. One of the guests at lunch was a Chinese executive whose company had just released a new film titled *China's Schindlers*. As the Chinese equivalent of the movie *Schindler's List*, this film was about the Chinese diplomat, Ho Feng Shan, who saved the lives of 5,000 Jews during World War II. Barry spoke with the Chinese executive at length about the film, and the two became friends.

A few weeks later, this Chinese executive was in Sydney on business and called Barry to meet. Barry asked him if he had ever visited a Jewish synagogue. When he replied he had not, Barry arranged for him and his delegation to visit a synagogue where Barry knew the rabbi.

At the synagogue, the rabbi brought out the Torah for them to read together. "The rabbi started talking about the synergies and similarities between Chinese and Jewish cultures, going back thousands of years." They noted, for example, that Hebrew is written from right to left and that Chinese is also written from right to left. The delegates were all very impressed by the rabbi's knowledge of and appreciation for their respective cultures.

At one point. the group also talked about the film *China's Schindlers*. At this time, two of the congregants at the synagogue politely approached the rabbi and the group. They explained they couldn't help but overhear the conversation about the film. They shared how their parents were two of the people that Ho Feng Shan had saved from the Nazis and how their families and this chance encounter at the synagogue would not have been possible without the actions of that brave diplomat!

As an Ambassador, he found common ground between the Chinese and Jewish cultures, including the impact of the brave actions of Ho Feng Shan, their 5,000+ year histories, their common values around family, education, and tradition, and even how they write and read the same way (that is, from right to left). Where one might look at the two cultures and see nothing but vast differences, he found many meaningful similarities. He does this all the time as an Ambassador.

These and other such experiences in building bridges—forming trusted, meaningful relationships across social boundaries—have led him to a twenty-year career in diplomacy and business between China and Australia. He has enabled countless interactions between the two countries, with journalists, government officials, and business leaders alike, and he continues to be a sought-after expert on Chinese culture, business, and contacts.

Barry the Explorer

As an explorer, he was used to traveling around the world, whether for business or pleasure, and he could make himself and others around him comfortable very quickly. His travels have included various countries in Africa, the Middle East, Asia, and North and South America. Writing about all his travels and the various communities he has been a part of would take more pages than we have room for here. So, I'll share one story from about twenty years ago when he was in Pakistan for business.

He was in Pakistan to build a software development outsourcing business, just as was already happening in India. This was a massive opportunity, and Barry needed to meet with and convince one particular Pakistani minister who was the key decision-maker for this project.

Barry noted, "I was quite young at the time, but I'm a Jewish guy, and I'm being invited to go to Pakistan, and we're going deep into Muslim territory." Talk about crossing social boundaries! Of course, there have been periods of tension between Jewish and Muslim communities, particularly in the context of the Israeli-Palestinian conflict. While Barry had no reason to think this minister would have any animosity toward him due to his heritage, he was also mindful that there are not many Jews in Pakistan, and it might be difficult for him to find common ground from which to build rapport with this man.

Barry had a friend who knew the minister and brokered an introduction, leading to a thirty-minute car ride in the minister's private car. Barry wondered to himself what he could possibly speak with this man about for thirty minutes! He quickly connected the dots and had an epiphany: "In Pakistan, their other religion is cricket, right? And I was a big cricket player when I was a kid!" So they talked about cricket, Australian cricket players, Pakistani cricket players, and so on. Thirty minutes later, they were fast friends.

Let's pause here to consider a few key points about how Barry is operating as an Explorer.

Barry leveraged an existing relationship (his friend) to get to the person he needed to speak with (the Pakistani minister). More often than not, when Barry enters a new community, he finds an ally (Advocate) from that community. In Pakistan, he asked his Pakistani

Australian friend for help, just like he did in China when he got help from his friend, who was the Chairman of the international bank.

Barry then had to find common ground with the minister. No two cultures could potentially be more opposed and fraught with danger than Jews and Muslims, with thousands of years of antagonism, mistrust, and war. Barry found a very human common interest in cricket, thereby forging a trusted bond of friendship that allowed everything else to take place.

Barry warned that as an Explorer, "at some point, you get tested by the locals." This is an observation shared by many of the other Explorers I've met, including Beth Dochnger. In Pakistan, Barry remembers riding with another influential executive. The man was driving Barry in his car at night on the freeway with the headlights turned off. At one point, he pulled over and asked Barry to do the same thing. Barry agreed and drove for he didn't know how long, with the headlights still turned off. Afterward, the man made all the introductions for Barry that were crucial for his goals. Explorers often have to brave certain tests to earn the trust of the locals!

Barry the Seer

This next story showcases Barry's expertise as a Seer. I noted he must have brought something else to the conversation with the Pakistani minister besides just cricket. You can put someone else in the car who is equally friendly and excited about cricket, and while that might lead to a great thirty-minute conversation about cricket, it easily could have stopped there. What else did Barry bring to the conversation that made the Pakistani minister want to work with him on the software development outsourcing business?

Barry answered matter-of-factly and without ego how he "painted for him a clear, compelling vision of how this could all turn out." He based this vision on his various insights about technology, the global economy, and market and labor conditions that would make this a successful venture for Pakistan. When I asked him where he got these insights, Barry's response was reminiscent of what Eric Larsen said

(Chapter 6). Barry said he speaks with many people and reads voraciously. He explained, "I've now been in so many different environments of so many different things. I can usually say something very interesting and relevant to talk to people about, and I can usually bring a fresh perspective, a different take on things that they hadn't heard before."

Barry is intuitively a Seer. He is constantly connecting the dots across many conversations he's having with a variety of people from many different domains, nationalities, and roles. He is constantly learning, and as he does so, he can offer new insights and new ways of looking at a topic to whomever he is speaking with.

Barry the Catalyst

Chances are, Barry embodies other archetypes, too. For example, he is likely a Catalyst who drives massive change and makes things happen. His career is full of big deals and initiatives that took place because of his efforts. As noted earlier, he is currently the Chairman of EQ Capital Partners. Here is the company description: "EQ Capital Partners is a private investment group working with long-term trusted global investment partners to deliver positive social impact and quality investment outcomes. We seek to invest in and partner with globally focused high-quality teams based on a relationship of ethics, trust, and shared values using an investment framework that tightly manages risk and maps outcomes explicitly to UN Sustainable Development Goals and other social impact investment metrics."

Barry the Sage

You put all that together into one person, and this is where you get the wisdom and expertise of a *Sage*. He can bring all his skills to bear at the same time. He doesn't think, *Okay, I'm now a Seer, and I'm going to synthesize information from the conversations I had last week*, and then switch to, *Okay, now I'm an Explorer, and I will go and meet these new people, talk about cricket, and become friends*. He just does it; it's all a core part of who he is.

The abilities of the various Super Connector archetypes blend into one with Barry, making him an incredibly effective Super Connector, bridge builder, explorer, seer, catalyst, and humanitarian. For someone so accomplished, he is affable, unassuming, self-deprecating, respectful, and genuinely curious about everyone he meets.

At the end of our interview, Barry asked a great question: "How do others do it?" How do other Super Connectors maintain so many relationships across so many domains? For Barry, he said it's all in his head. He uses some technology (his phone, address book, and so on), but the details of relationships are primarily in his head.

Surprisingly, my interviews have not yet yielded any great, revolutionary answers to this question. Nevertheless, in the next two chapters about energy and technology, I explore ways in which Super Connectors do what they do "at scale" and over long periods of time, along with the tools they use.

CHAPTER 13:
ENERGY MANAGEMENT

"We must never become too busy sawing to take time to sharpen the saw."
~ Stephen Covey, The 7 Habits of Highly Effective People ~

W e live in an energy-deficient world right now, and I don't mean the world consumes more energy than it produces, although according to the World Bank, 13 percent of the world's population does not have access to electricity, and 40 percent of the world does not have access to clean fuels for cooking.[1]

I'm referring more to the fact that we, as individuals and as a collection of individuals, live lives so packed with urgent tasks, endless meetings, and a series of to-dos that we have little to no free time and are, as a result, constantly on the verge of collapse. In China, they have a phrase called "996," which stands for working from 9:00 am to 9:00 pm, six days a week. The global COVID-19 pandemic forced people to work from home, which made it easier to take video meetings at all hours of the day, extending people's work hours into early mornings, evenings, and weekends. Is it any surprise the World Economic Forum has declared lack of sleep as a global epidemic, with about 62 percent of adults saying they're not getting enough sleep?

In this context, taking time out for yourself can be difficult, whether it's quality time spent with family and friends, regular time for exercise, hiking, meditation, or just downtime to read or think. If it's this difficult to find time for *yourself*, how much more difficult is it for Super Connectors to make time for *others*?

Consider that Super Connectors are *givers* who often give their time, attention, and effort without asking for anything back. For example, as a rule, Eric Larsen (Chapter 6) has nine conversations with a client where he adds value before he has one where he asks for something back. Super Connectors are "giving" like this across hundreds, if not thousands, of relationships. That's a lot of time and effort!

Also, consider how the act of connecting is an energy-intensive activity. Connecting with others, making meaningful connections for others, bringing people into communities, and so on, all require focused mental and emotional energy. These are not activities one can do mindlessly. According to the Leadership Institute for Tomorrow (LIFT):

> "Making a connection with others requires energy, patience, selflessness, clarity, and initiative. These are all indicators of a person who gives during a communication exchange. They are interesting and engaging, speaking slowly and clarifying as necessary so others understand. They are prepared, personable, and passionate… The leader who communicates with their people from a position of appreciation, passion, compassion, and grace are in a giving mode. This positive energy flows outward, renewing and motivating others."

So, how do Super Connectors find the time and energy to do what they do? What do they do specifically to sustain and recharge themselves so they can do what they do over time?

Super Connectors Love What They Do

For Super Connectors, meeting people, making introductions, bringing people into communities, seeing patterns, exploring different worlds, and so forth, are all things they love to do. For example, my friend Sparrow Mahoney (an Explorer) loves to travel the world and meet all kinds of people and makes unusual and amazing connections as a result. Doing what they do comes to them as naturally as breathing, thinking, and feeling. It's their natural way of being.

An essential corollary to this is that you can't fake this, at least not for long. If you are not a giver, and if you don't like making connections for others and bringing people together, then it's difficult if not impossible to be a Super Connector.

Super Connectors are Often Recharged by What They Do

When done right, their activities deliver an inherent and intrinsic reward to the Super Connector. The extroverted Superhost may get charged up by spending time with friends over a nice meal. The introverted Seer may be deeply satisfied when she derives new insights from her recent one-on-one conversations with people. The Explorer is often happiest being "out there" and meeting new people in unfamiliar settings. The Community Builder relishes the sense of belonging created by the community she cultivates, and so on. These intrinsic rewards help to sustain a Super Connector's efforts over time.

It's About Managing Energy, Not Just Time

In his landmark book *The 7 Habits of Highly Effective People*, Stephen Covey writes about the seventh habit, which he calls "to sharpen the saw." The idea is that for people to be effective long-term, they must proactively make the time to replenish themselves, even invest in themselves.

Almost every Super Connector I've spoken with has a keen sense of what they individually need to recharge, and they proactively make the time to do so. Making the time to recharge is the only way that they can *be* a Super Connector. If you cannot sustain this activity over a long period of time, then you won't have the depth and breadth of the relationships, nor the scale and strength of communities, to be a Super Connector. The only way to sustain yourself like this is to proactively make time to recharge yourself.

Based on a survey of the more than 150 Super Connectors I've met, here are some helpful insights:

- *Exercise* was the most popular way to recharge. It didn't matter what the exercise was, only that they regularly got off their chairs and did something physical.
- *Mindfulness* and **gratitude** help. Many Super Connectors also practiced mindfulness exercises, such as meditation. Another respondent shared, "I take regular pauses for 'Glad To Be Here' big-picture positive reflections. I also work on keeping a positive mindset, and having a positive voice in my head, such as 'let the noise pass,' 'stay focused,' and 'have fun with it.'"
- *Time of day matters*. Super Connectors were aware they have different times throughout the day when they are more energetic, and are also aware there are times when it's easier for them to make connections. The time of day varied from person to person. For example, one interviewee shared, "I cherish a solid one or two hours in the morning with coffee and my thoughts to get solitary work done and ramped up for the day." They were aware of when they are at their best being a Super Connector versus working on a presentation versus going through emails, for example.
- Even extroverts need *downtime*. While the extroverted Super Connectors noted (happily) how these activities actually charge them up, they, too, needed downtime and rest to recharge. "Fallow" time to recharge is critical.

There is a great *Harvard Business Review* article from 2007 that talks about the importance of energy management versus time management. This passage nicely summarizes the whole article:

"The core problem with working longer hours is that time is a finite resource. Energy is a different story. Defined in physics as the capacity to work, energy comes from four main wellsprings in human beings: the body, emotions, mind, and spirit. In each, energy can be systematically expanded and regularly renewed by establishing specific rituals—behaviors that are intentionally practiced and precisely scheduled, with the goal of making them unconscious and automatic as quickly as possible."

They Leverage Other Super Connectors

Super Connectors know (whether intuitively or consciously) that they need other Super Connectors to succeed. We've seen many examples of this in the previous chapters. Catalysts can partner with Community Builders and Advocates to leverage a community and identify the experts required for the Catalyst's mission. The Explorer finds local Advocates to help them fit in and find the people and resources they seek. The Community Builder needs the Elder to help maintain the identity and values of the community, and the Seer to know what changes are necessary to adapt and grow the community. As we'll see in a later chapter, Super Connectors often connect in networks of their own to support one another. Trying to do all this on your own is way too difficult and time-consuming, if not outright impossible (even for the Sage).

They Leverage Communities

Super Connectors intuitively or consciously know how to leverage communities to help sustain their efforts. Recall that Anna Morgenstern leverages the communities around her to see how her clients are at social situations. Ryan Groves (Chapter 5) built communities in college to create a sense of belonging for himself and others. Bob Stone (Chapter 7) brings together people from various backgrounds into a community to collectively invent brand new products and services. Super Connectors build, leverage, and work with communities of people to help sustain what they do.

They Make it a Habit

The most successful Super Connectors have built-in habits that make it easier for them to be more effective over time. Eric Larsen said, "I've constructed my schedule," including reserving 25 hours each week to simply "learn." Michael Roderick, another prolific Super Connector, writes blogs about relationships every day and shares them with his community. Rebecca Friese held her "12 at 12" luncheons *monthly*. Whether it's making time to reach out to people one-on-one, bringing people together into communities, or making regular time for travel, Super Connectors make their core activities as habitual as possible.

They Use Systems and Technology to Connect at Scale

In the next chapter, let's consider how Super Connectors use technology to help them scale their efforts over time.

Chapter 13 Notes

1. See https://ourworldindata.org/energy-access.
2. See LIFT source
3. See https://hbr.org/2007/10/manage-your-energy-not-your-time.

CHAPTER 14:
TECHNOLOGY ENABLERS

"Technology is nothing. What's important is that you have faith in people, that they're basically good and smart, and if you give them tools, they'll do wonderful things with them."
~ Steve Jobs ~

Bill's Story

We begin this chapter with a story about Bill. Starting from when he was in college, Bill made it a point to write down information about the people he met on three-by-five index cards. He would include personal information about the individual, such as their family, hobbies, work, and so on. At the end of each day, Bill would meticulously jot down all this information onto his index cards to help him remember because, as bright as he was, he knew he couldn't remember everything. Whenever he had a call or met with someone again, he would update the relevant information on the relevant index card.

Over time, he added to his collection of index cards. His relationships included college friends, neighbors, senators, business and civic leaders, scientists, celebrities, and other luminaries worldwide. Eventually, he was able to leverage his many connections to become the forty-second President of the United States! This is the story of President William Jefferson Clinton. By the time he was elected, he had amassed a collection of more than *ten thousand* such index cards.[1]

The point here is not that having a network of ten thousand names will get you to become a Super Connector or to a position of power, nor is it to say we should all go around with a pen and index cards to jot down everything we learn about the people we meet. Instead, the point of Bill's story is to illustrate the challenge Super Connectors face in trying to keep track of everyone they know and all the relevant details about them. The "technology" solution can be as simple as good old-fashioned 3x5 index cards, or as complex as sophisticated Personal Relationship Management (PRM) software. Either way, the challenge is the same.

To sum it up, here are the challenges Super Connectors face when trying to keep track of all their relationships:

- *Effectively keeping track of all the details about everyone you know:* This includes facts such as birthdays and other special occasions, family members, work, and so forth.
- *Keeping track of all your moments of engagement*: When did we first meet, and what were all the times after that? When did we last meet, and what did we talk about? We don't have to remember every detail, but we should recall the important conversations, get-togethers, and so on.
- *Keeping track of the connections you've made for that person:* This is not to keep track of favors, but to be more keenly aware of the developing/deepening relationships around you. Plus, you don't want to make the same introduction as if you've never introduced them before!
- *Keeping track of the major changes in people's lives:* Did they get a new job, move to a new city, win an award, get married, or have a new child?
- *Receiving proactive reminders of their special occasions:* These would include birthdays, anniversaries, and so on.
- *Sending them relevant information:* This might be an article or note showing them you were thinking about them at that time.

The real challenge is doing this *at scale*. It's not difficult to do this with the people we care about the most. Think about your family members (spouse, parents, grandparents, siblings, cousins, and so forth). Chances are good that you remember all kinds of facts about them, you know what's going on in their lives, and it's not difficult to remember to send them a thoughtful gift here and there. The same thing applies to your closest friends. The challenge is to do this at scale with hundreds, thousands, maybe even tens of thousands of people. How does one do *that*?

For most humans, it's impossible to do this at scale without help because most of us don't have perfect memory. Even if we had a photographic memory and could recall every detail about everyone we know at will, we simply don't have enough time in the day to proactively reach out to hundreds of people. This is where technology comes in because it can help scale what we do.

It's important to emphasize how technology is *not* a substitute for real human connections. As Christine Lai, another Super Connector, put it, "Technology is not a primary way to stay in touch. It does not maintain the true and real level of the connection." Just having a connection with someone on LinkedIn or Facebook does not make that person your friend.

Eric Larsen (Chapter 6) advised, "To me, it's about being intentional about the relationship. Put the effort into connecting and go into it with an open mind, but also with a plan. What do they want, and what do I want to give?" Technology cannot be a replacement for the intention and effort required to genuinely connect with other people; it is simply an aid to help us to *scale* that effort. While the previous chapter on energy management was about how to sustain the effort *over time,* this chapter is more about how to *scale* the effort across thousands of relationships.

It may seem tedious, unglamorous, or even calculating to keep track of people's information like this. We don't have to do this with the people we genuinely care about, like our family and close friends, so isn't it fake and manipulative to do all this and pretend we care about these other people?

The key word here is *care*. Recall that Super Connectors are givers. They care about other people and want to contribute. You might not be their closest friend, but they *do* genuinely care. If they didn't care, they would not put in the effort to keep track of information about you.

Also, consider what it feels like to be on the receiving side of that effort. What does it feel like when someone remembers who you are and what you care about? What does it feel like when someone sends you a birthday card (do people even still do that?) or a nice email saying, "Hey, I was thinking about you, and here's something you might want to read." The time and effort taken to do this *shows* they care, and these small interactions add up to a lot over time.

So, how do Super Connectors use technology nowadays to scale what they do? Are there any secret tools Super Connectors use to be more effective?

I polled the various Super Connectors I interviewed, and below are the results. The question was: What tools do you use to help you keep track of and manage your relationships? I then had a list of possibilities and asked them to check all the ones that applied to them.

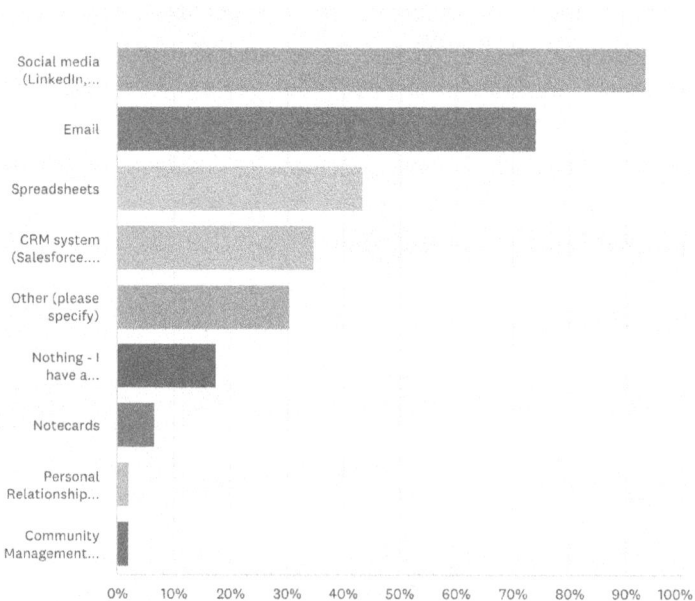

Here are some key observations about the use of technology among the Super Connectors I surveyed:

First, and sadly, there is no "magic bullet" or single tool Super Connectors use to be more effective. To be clear, while there are many software products out there that purport to help in various ways, there was no obvious winner with all of the features and functionality needed for the job. One interviewee noted, "I wish I had access to better tools for managing relationships as I'm sure I'd be so much more effective." Instead, Super Connectors have to resort to a variety of tools, with limited and mixed results.

Second, more than 90 percent of the respondents use Social Media platforms such as LinkedIn and Facebook to stay connected with others. This is good news for those service providers, and it's certainly easy to digitally "connect" with friends and colleagues using these tools. That said, there are certain downsides to this particular technology. For one, you are limited by the service's functionality, which does not differentiate based on the strength of the relationships. You also have to sift through a lot of noise on these platforms, such as unsolicited messages, advertisements, phishing attacks, and so on.

Email is the second most common way to stay connected. Email has continued to be surprisingly useful for a technology invented in 1978 and one that many other tools have tried to replace. It is the *lingua franca* of electronic communication, and you can reach most people by email in ways you can't with other tools. Still, it's only a communication tool, not a relationship management platform, that can help you keep track of information about your contacts.

This is where Super Connectors often use spreadsheets. Spreadsheets are a quick and easy way to keep track of contacts with relevant information such as names, facts, dates, and so forth. Think of it like an electronic version of the three-by-five index cards. One interviewee noted, "Google Sheets specifically seems to work best for me in terms of flexibility, ease of use, exporting, and sharing capabilities." That said, spreadsheets lack the functionality to help you be proactive about reaching out to people and can also be error-prone.

Other communication tools, such as WhatsApp, are cheap and easy alternatives, but they can be difficult to navigate, especially with a lot of members. While they're useful for communication, they're not really helpful for managing and keeping track of relevant information about the people (apart from their names, phone numbers, and maybe a small photo).

What about Customer Relationship Management (CRM) systems? In the business world, there are plenty of CRM systems, from Microsoft Dynamics and Salesforce.com's Sales Cloud to the more lightweight and cheaper tools such as Insightly, Zoho, and AirTable. They are mostly designed for salespeople to keep track of sales opportunities and convert them to closed deals. There is functionality for keeping track of people's information, but that's not much better than a spreadsheet. What's missing is a more proactive way to be alerted. As a side note, I personally find AirTable to be an effective mix of both spreadsheets and a lightweight CRM system.

Notecards? Yes! Surprisingly, a number of the respondents supplement digital technology with good old fashioned pen-and-paper. Others use electronic notecards (such as Evernote) or other note-taking tools such as Google Docs to jot down notes about people.

Way down on the list is a category called Personal Relationship Management (PRM) software. These are tools similar to CRM systems but designed for personal use, theoretically making it easier for people like Super Connectors to track and manage their personal relationships. That said, this is still a small market with many small vendors and no clear leader.

So, where does this leave us on the technology/tools front?

The world is already full of technology, and I would argue we are suffocating under their weight. We are attached to our mobile devices and often have multiple screens on at the same time in the same room. These devices all have many applications running on them, all of which are carefully designed and calibrated to capture your attention and have you react to their pings, urgent notifications, and requests for action. Social media applications also have us trapped in social echo chambers of "like-minded" people and friends, where we are supposed to connect with friends but end up isolating ourselves from the rest of the world. We don't really need more technology; we probably need less.

That said, if Steve Jobs is right, then the *right* technology can be a useful tool for Super Connectors to make their lives easier and their connecting more effective. This is not about creating or using more technology, but about thinking through the right tool or set of tools to help Super Connectors with their scaling challenges, while also freeing them to focus on what they do best. I argue there are six key features for such a technology:

1. Keep track of facts about people.
2. Keep track of moments of engagement with people.
3. Keep track of people's updates from social media, news, and so on.
4. Be proactive in reaching out to them (for anniversaries and so forth).
5. Help prioritize!
6. Make it easy to use.

Any takers? Please let me know!

We end this chapter with the story of a Super Connector who famously does *not* rely on technology—just stories—to keep track of her many relationships.

Elizabeth Patterson

Elizabeth Patterson is the Partner for People and Talent at the Silicon Valley venture capital firm Sapphire Ventures. If she has an eye for talent, then she also has an ear for people's stories, which she says is the key to her ability to remember relevant and personal details about so many people.

Elizabeth grew up in the Midwest in a fairly idyllic environment. Her father, a college professor, was from Wisconsin, and her mother, an elementary school teacher, was from Wyoming. They would go to Church on Sundays, her brother was an Eagle Scout, and they always had friends and family over for gatherings.

She credits her parents for her Super Connector skills. "In our family, we have the midwestern DNA about the importance of family, relationships, neighborhoods, and community" she explained. She watched her parents build relationships with everyone around them including students, faculty, neighbors, fellow church goers, and many others.

She said that she has always been "insanely curious" about people, just as her parents were, and that she always loved to hear people's stories. She fondly remembers hours spent listening to her grandparents tell stories about her extended family, and to this day, she loves hearing people's stories about themselves and their lives.

This is how she found she is able to effortlessly recall details about so many people. "What I grip onto and remember about people are their stories. Stories enable me to connect to people, and I have an almost photographic memory about people and the many random facts that make them who they are, all because of their stories!" she explained.

Humans are hardwired to think in terms of stories. That is how we make sense of the world around us. Stories light up more parts of our brains, and as our neurons fire, they form more connections, thus helping us to remember more details from these stories. The emotional component of stories further helps us strengthen those connections and thus our recall. Dr. Jennifer Aaker in the Stanford Graduate School of Business has explained that, as a result, "a story is up to twenty-two times more memorable than facts alone."[2]

Both in and out of work, Elizabeth is constantly making connections for people. As the head of People and Talent at her firm, she and her team are responsible for finding the best possible talent for their portfolio companies, matching up candidates with startups not just based on their skills but also their culture fit. She also connects the leaders from their portfolio companies to other experts around the world who can be helpful with their startups' growth and success. No doubt she uses email, messaging apps, and other tools to help her with her efforts, but the vast majority of the details about all the people she knows she keeps in her wonderful stories about them!

So what happens when Super Connectors are able to sustain and scale their efforts over time? How large a reach can Super Connectors have? In the next chapter, you'll read stories about two "Super Connectors of Super Connectors" to help illustrate what's possible when this power is leveraged at scale.

Chapter 14 Notes

1. See https://getdex.com/blog/networking-journey-to-the-oval-office.
2. See https://leanin.org/education/harnessing-the-power-of-stories.

CHAPTER 15:
CONNECTING WITH OTHER SUPER CONNECTORS

"If you want to go fast, go alone; if you want to go far, go together."
~ Anonymous ~

David Homan

I t's November 1, 2017, in New York City. It's a balmy Wednesday evening with temperatures in the mid-fifties. You have an invitation from David Homan for you and other "Connectors" to gather at 7:00 pm at the Gansevoort Hotel in Chelsea.

One of David's rules is that you have to be on time. He explained, "I believe in punctuality for many reasons, but primarily, it's about respect for other people's time. More broadly, they have to come in the spirit of giving. It's not about what they will get from the event, but who they could give to."

So, you show up a bit early. Promptly at 7:00 pm, the door closes to the private room, and David kicks off the event. It's called *Orchestrated Connecting,* and it's the first of its kind.

David's Orchestrated Connecting is an example of a network of Super Connectors and illustrates what's possible when you bring such people together into a community. In this chapter, we explore Super Connectors of Super Connectors—people like David Homan and Adria Dunn—and the networks of Super Connectors they assemble.

At David's inaugural event in 2017, there were forty attendees, and everyone was a Super Connector in their own right. David's selection criteria for the people he invited were simple: "One, they all described themselves as super connectors; two, they have to be people I would trust my children with; and three, they have to be on time."

Today, David's Orchestrated Connecting community has more than 1,200 members worldwide. Below are some essential characteristics of the community.

Trust

Membership is by invitation only. David added, "You cannot buy your way into the community. You can only enter based on trust. That makes the network even more powerful and valuable." To increase that trust, he strictly maintains the selection criteria that the attendees must be high-integrity people.

Diversity

By intention, it's a very diverse group of people with respect to the attendees' gender, age, ethnicity, profession, socioeconomic background, and so on. David explains, "The diversity is purposeful, not just for the inclusion, but because it's the most strategic. As a Super Connector, you will make an introduction for someone outside of your communities only if it's strategic and important. And at the highest level of connectivity, that diversity is absolutely key to how Super Connectors work."

Gratitude

One of David's rules is that the community members must "honor the chain of connecting." This means that if something meaningful came out of a conversation you had with someone you met, then you have to honor the connection by thanking the people who made it possible, "five layers deep."

Why is this so important? David explained, "When you thank the chain of people who made the connection possible, it builds a community that works. The people making the connections are thus seen visibly for the outcomes of their introductions, and the value of those relationships and introductions are also made visible over time."

This is a problem David had been trying to solve for many years, and it's one most Super Connectors are well aware of. Before Orchestrated Connecting, he had been making introductions for others for years without acknowledgment, thanks, or follow-up. The requestor got what they wanted, and that was that. This lack of recognition and gratitude does not strengthen David's relationships in that context. Instead, this erodes the trust in the relationships and, cumulatively, destroys the community around the Super Connector.

Why is it just about giving thanks and not something else? David believes no other "currency" besides gratitude would work. Money is out of the question. If David had been paid for the introduction, it would fundamentally change the nature of the relationship and the connection, and it would not work after that. The most effective "payment" for the introduction is gratitude and the recognition of the Super Connector for what they made possible. The Super Connector is the super node in the network of our society, and by expressing gratitude to that person, we strengthen that node and all the relationships around the node.

Reach

David says you can reach pretty much anyone through this network. According to a number of studies, everyone on our planet is connected to each other not by six degrees of separation but by just 3.4 degrees.[1] In this context, Super Connectors are the super nodes that shorten the distance between people. Some are like Grand Central Terminal (New York City's main commuter rail terminal), connecting a lot of people locally, while others are like JFK International Airport, connecting a lot of people across vast distances. Because David's network is made up of such super nodes, they can reach almost anyone on Earth in just a couple of hops.

Purpose

What does one do with such a network of people? David has organized the community and its events to support the various impact initiatives of its members. The "ask" most people make in this group is not about making more money, increasing their social media profile, or growing their businesses. Instead, the "ask" is about the positive impact they strive to have in the world. Of course, they want to help each other to be commercially successful, but that is a byproduct of their impact initiatives. The community views everything through the lens of the positive impact they can have in society. "And that's how I built an intentional community of super connectors," David explained. For this, I am immensely grateful.

Let's now consider the story of another Super Connector of Super Connectors for comparison.

Adria Dunn

Adria is an incredible Super Connector who brings together family offices and high-net-worth individuals with nonprofits to help fund causes that make the world better. Her network, called the Vine, has more than 2,000 members worldwide, many of whom are Super Connectors themselves.

Adria has also worked with dozens of the community's members to publish a book titled *The Vine: Messages of Hope from Around the World*, which includes letters of hope from His Holiness the Dalai Lama, Dr. Jane Goodall, spiritual leader Gurudev Sri Sri Ravi Shankar, and HRH Princess Reema Bandar Al Saud (Saudi Arabia ambassador to the US), among other humanitarians and luminaries.

There are distinct similarities between how Adria and David organize and run their impact communities.

Trust

Adria very carefully screens everyone who joins her network to ensure they will be positive contributors to the community. Membership is by invitation only, and she "triple checks" everyone with back-channel references to ensure each one is a "person of high integrity who is there to contribute rather than just take." This creates an incredible environment of mutual respect and trust for everyone.

It's not just about getting in. There are essential guidelines for how to remain a member in good standing. For example, Adria is strict about this rule: You cannot promote your products or services. Break this rule (or any other rule) and you are out *forever*. This is not a community where you sell to each other. Instead, it's a community where you help each other make the world better.

Diversity

As a matter of privacy, I cannot share who is in the community, but I can attest that the members hail from all around the world and represent family offices, philanthropists, nonprofit leaders, social entrepreneurs, and other innovators working to make the world better for everyone. Many of these members self-identify as Super Connectors.

Purpose

As with David's Orchestrated Connecting, the purpose of the Vine is to do good in the world by supporting the impact initiatives of its members. Adria's book is an example of the kind of impact this community has in our world, with messages of hope directly from the membership.

Much more happens naturally, however, as the members share about their efforts in the various gatherings. For example, after the recent fires in Maui (August 2023), many of the members spontaneously organized themselves to help with donations and other resources. Countless other positive collaborations occur, all with Adria's blessing but few with her direct involvement. As a Community Builder, she curates the community, and the members take action.

Implications of Impact Networks

There are a few essential implications of such impact networks to consider in terms of what can happen when you have a network of Super Connectors.

First, these impact networks are very powerful, and we have yet to see what's truly possible when more of them organize, develop, and mature. As we saw in earlier chapters, communities have an inherent power to organize and take action. A community of Super Connectors has an incredible ability to reach other people all around the world, thus unleashing unforeseen capabilities and results. A "regular" community is limited to the members it has, whereas a community of Super Connectors has the distinct ability to expand and connect with almost anyone in the world.

Second, if you are a Super Connector (or aspire to be one), please consider joining forces with other Super Connectors in such impact networks. In the case of Super Connectors, I believe 1+1 = 11, and we can exponentially expand our reach and capabilities when we join forces with one another, especially in a community of our own. If you're looking for an intentional community of Super Connectors to join, please email gunil@superconnect.co !

Third, if you are a Super Connector who organizes and runs such a network, please recognize the responsibility you have to use this enormous power for good. As we'll see in our next and final chapter, the power a Super Connector wields can be used for "good" or "evil." You can use this power to build and nurture a community of 100,000 refugees from Nepal or to create the largest hate group in America. There aren't many people in the world who can do what you do, so please consider your power very carefully.

With that in mind, we turn now to our final chapter to consider why this book is titled Super Connector *Manifesto*.

Chapter 15 Notes

1. See https://en.wikipedia.org/wiki/Six_degrees_of_separation.

CHAPTER 16:
CONCLUSION ~ THE MANIFESTO

*"The only thing necessary for the triumph of evil is for good
[people] to do nothing."*
~ Anonymous ~

D uring one of my conversations with my friends about this book, someone asked me if it's possible to have a Super Connector who uses their powers for evil. Given how powerful and effective Super Connectors can be in bringing people into communities and in marshaling the resources of that community toward a goal, what happens if they do so with an evil motive? Even if not an overtly evil motive, then what about at least a hidden selfish agenda designed to serve their personal gain rather than the well-being of the community and its members?

My first reaction was, "No way!" All the Super Connectors I met were givers, genuinely curious about people, and motivated by a strong desire to help others. There was no way I could imagine any of them doing something hurtful toward others, at least not consciously or for long, let alone doing something actively harmful to the world around them.

I then thought, however, about some of the greatest atrocities committed in the world, such as the rise of the Nazis in World War II and the Holocaust. Who were the connectors during that time which helped a fringe political group organize, grow, and consolidate power as the Nazis?

How about the Ku Klux Klan? Did you know there were between three and eight million members of the KKK in the 1920s? At the time, there were only about 115 million people living in the US, which means about seven percent of the population were members of the KKK! The Klan had devised a strategy called "the decade," where every member was responsible for recruiting ten people to vote for Klan candidates in local elections. This and other efforts led the Klan to dominate local and state politics from coast to coast, including the mayors of Portland, Maine, and Portland, Oregon.[1] In some states, such as Colorado and Indiana, they succeeded in placing enough Klansmen in positions of power to effectively control the state government.[2] Also known as the "Invisible Empire," the KKK's presence and impact were felt across the US.

What about the secret cells organized by terrorist groups? In *The Future of Terrorism*, John Picarelli, the Director of the US Department of Homeland Security Center for Prevention Programs and Partnerships, wrote about how terrorist leaders recruit and organize people into their organizations. Similarly, Professor Kjell Hausken of the University of Stavanger in Norway, in his 2019 paper titled *The dynamics of terrorist organizations*, wrote about ideologues who "provide political purpose and direction and have a strong group commitment."[3] They "ensure the ideological commitment, and may sacrifice their own interests and even their lives for the organization." They are writing about Super Connectors!

I began this book by saying the major challenges we face in the world are not technology or policy problems but social problems rooted in our inability to come together across social differences, find common ground, develop a common solution, and take collective action. Super Connectors are, by definition, people who are well-suited to help us to address these challenges.

What becomes evident as we explore this topic is that this power can be used for both "good" or "evil," and there have been—and continue to be—those who use this power to commit heinous acts against others.

I'm not here to debate what is "good" or "evil." There are some things that are clearly evil, such as the genocide of millions of Jews, the systematic oppression and enslavement of millions of minorities, war crimes that target innocent civilians, and so on. There are, however, many other things people can argue are "good" or "evil," depending on their point of view.

Again, my goal here is not to debate what is good or evil. Instead, my goal here is to make this point: As Super Connectors, you have a responsibility to use your powers for the greater good. Yes, there are people already out there using the power and techniques of a Super Connector to cause harm. In that context, you have a clear choice: to either use your powers for good to help those around you or to do nothing.

I also ask you this: If you don't, who will? If Lorine Pendleton (Chapter 8) doesn't advocate for minority entrepreneurs, who will? If Shiva Sapkota (Chapter 11) hadn't helped the other refugees from Nepal, would such a thriving community exist in the US today? If Carlito Rofoli (Chapter 11) hadn't befriended so many other dancers, would the West Coast Swing community be as global as it is today? If Arno Michaelis (Chapter 9) doesn't regularly cross into the white supremacist community, who will help heal those wounds of hatred? If Nora Paxton (Chapter 3) doesn't bring her friends together into her home, who will create a hearth for them? If Robert Swan (Chapter 10) doesn't travel the world, who will advocate for the Antarctic? As is often said, "The only thing necessary for the triumph of evil is for good people to do nothing."

I used to think that someone else—someone in a position of greater power, wealth, and responsibility—would address and solve the world's challenges. Whether it would be the President of the United States, the members of the United Nations, the leaders of organizations such as the World Economic Forum, the executives of nonprofits such as the Gates Foundation, or other civic and social leaders, surely *someone else* would use their positions and powers to solve the challenges we all face.

I've come to see, however, that this line of thinking is not enough. Yes, we need all the good men and women in positions of power to continue to do their work, and it's not enough. The world is not getting safer and more peaceful. The climate crisis is not getting better. The Great Pacific Garbage Patch is not going away and is instead becoming a small continent. The economic disparity between the haves and have-nots is increasing. Racial tensions and gun violence continue to roil our communities.

Furthermore, it's impossible for any one person, no matter how brave, smart, motivated, or powerful, to tackle these challenges alone. We must act together, and Super Connectors have a unique power to bring people together to enable collective action.

The world has lived with the narrative of the "Hero's Journey" for too long. Popularized by Joseph Campbell, we live in a world suffused with the idea that there is a singular being who can vanquish evil and save the day. That could be Superman, Ironman, Neo in the Matrix trilogy, Luke Skywalker, Captain Marvel, or Wonder Woman. Or it could be the Mayor, a Governor, the President, the CEO of a nonprofit, or a billionaire entrepreneur. Or maybe it's a superstar athlete, musician, or film personality. They may all be incredible human beings doing great work, but they all represent the narrative of the Hero's Journey.

I assert that the world now needs a new narrative, one that my friend Dave Zaboski calls the "Kindred Quest." This is more in line with *Star Trek*—yes, with a Captain, but also a team of people to help carry out the mission. Or *The Fellowship of the Ring* with a ragtag group of adventurers united in their mission to defeat the evil Sauron, brought together by Gandalf, the great Super Connector! We need more stories illustrating the narrative of the Kindred Quest, where only *collectively* can a group of heroes achieve their goal. I assert that in each of these stories of the Kindred Quest, there is a Super Connector who brings everyone together.

Ultimately, in the fight betweeen "good" versus "evil," I believe good triumphs. Evil might be ascendant for a period of time (as we've seen with the Nazis), but good will eventually prevail. Why? Because society needs its members to look after the greater good for the society itself to survive, let alone thrive. Actions that hurt many in service of the few will eventually fail because the results are not sustainable for society, which would then die. So, in order for society to grow and thrive, we need actions that bring about the greatest good possible to as many people as possible.

This does not, however, happen automatically. We must all make the choice, both individually and collectively, to take actions we believe will benefit not just us alone but others also. What is the greatest good we can bring into the world?

Fundamentally, this choice is based on the realization that we're not just better together; we're actually all one. As Arno Michaelis so eloquently put it:

> "The root cause of all of the issues we face together as a human race is a disconnect from each other's humanity – an inability, in short, to have compassion for one another and ourselves. This is a spiritual problem that requires a spiritual solution, not a political one. That spiritual solution is found in service and oneness, as demonstrated by the Sikh community after the shooting at the temple in Wisconsin."[4]

In the course of these pages, I hope I was able to show how you, as a Super Connector, can help. What started out as an exploration of what it means to be a Super Connector has morphed into a Manifesto, a call for you to be who you are and to help bring the world together.

First, this requires us to recognize and own our powers as Super Connectors. Too many of us toil away at organizations where our traits and skills are not fully appreciated and where the job does not fully leverage our powers. Eric Larsen strongly advises we double down on our strengths and "become indispensable" by fully owning and maximizing our talents.

Second, we must help each other develop our skills as Super Connectors. Each archetype has a special set of skills and practices others do not have, and there is an opportunity for us to help each other to learn and grow.

Third, we must look beyond the day-to-day details of our jobs and lives to see how we can help unite the world. Maybe you're already in such a job, and that's great. How can you partner with other Super Connectors and communities to expand your reach and impact? Or maybe there is an opportunity to redefine your role to better utilize your skills as a Super Connector. Or maybe you can volunteer or partner with an organization like Greenhouse (dba as Greenhouse Scholars) to help teach and support others to be better community builders and leaders.[5]

Fourth, if we are really ambitious, we could connect with other Super Connectors in Impact Networks to help take collective action towards causes that we care about. Imagine a global network of Super Connectors!

Fifth, and maybe most importantly, we must model and live the values of being a Super Connector in our daily lives. We can show compassion and love to our fellow brothers and sisters on earth, no matter the social constructs around us. We can approach relationships with curiosity and the intent to give rather than take. We can seek to understand, especially those whose viewpoints we disagree with. Imagine if our actions inspired others to do the same!

In the face of all that is happening in the world, what do we choose? Do we choose to do nothing, to just give up and assume someone else will do it? I hope instead you will choose to be who you are, a Super Connector, and help bring the world together.

Chapter 16 Notes

1. See https://digitalcommons.library.umaine.edu/cgi/viewcontent.cgi?article=1223&context=mainehistory and https://digitalcommons.chapman.edu/cgi/viewcontent.cgi?article=1126&context=vocesnovae.

2. See https://www.governing.com/archive/when-the-klan-ran.html and https://www.in.gov/library/collections-and-services/indiana/subject-guides-to-indiana-collection-materials/ku-klux-klan-in-indiana/.
3. See https://www.sciencedirect.com/science/article/pii/S2214716018303385.
4. See https://www.cnn.com/2017/08/15/opinions/ex-white-power-compassion-answer-michaelis-opinion/index.html.
5. https://greenhousescholars.org.

FREQUENTLY ASKED QUESTIONS

1. **Are Super Connectors all extroverted?**

   Absolutely not. In my research and interviews, I've found no correlation between being a Super Connector and being an extrovert. In fact, some of the archetypes (such as the Seer) are often quite introverted. Instead, Super Connectors *combine* the powers of both introverts and extroverts to do what they do.

2. **Are Super Connectors all people in positions of power?**

   The relationship between Super Connectors and power is fascinating. It's certainly true that people in positions of power have vast and powerful networks of their own, and they usually work hard to maintain and grow their networks.

   Super Connectors, however, are often not in positions of power in the traditional sense. In fact, as you've read in the preceding chapters, they often *avoid* the spotlight and prefer to work behind the scenes. More importantly, Super Connectors wield a different kind of power, one that is renewable and almost limitless, which I call Community Power.

   Community Power is different from the *positional power* of a CEO or the President of the US where the position itself grants the individual *access* to a vast network. It's also different from *network power*, where a network is leveraged in order to *rise to power*.

   Super Connectors work with communities. Super Connectors can create and/or leverage various communities of people, and these communities have an inherent power to act, especially when mobilized by a Catalyst toward a mission or purpose. In this book,

I'm far more interested in how Super Connectors create and leverage *Community Power* because it is not dependent on positional power, nor is it about rising to positions of power. It is about the ability of Super Connectors to mobilize groups of people into a community and create power that did not exist before within that community.

You'll see that Super Connectors often give up control to create their communities. They lead in a different way, through influence and stewardship, through the moral mandate given to them by the community. The community members look to the Super Connector to make decisions in the best interest of the community, and to help maintain the culture intact and consistent. Super Connectors take on power lightly with their communities, and I argue we need more of this form of power going forward.

And there is no limit to Community Power. Benjamin Franklin created a formidable and influential community (the Leather Apron Club) that eventually became the American Philosophical Society. What if we could do that a million times? And because anyone can do this if they choose to—regardless of the position or power they have in society—there is no practical limit to the number of communities that could be created. Imagine what's possible!

3. Are Super Connectors born that way, or can this be learned?

My observation is that most of this is learned. To be sure, Super Connectors are often born with natural tendencies that make it easier for them to learn the traits and skills to become great at it. For example, many of my interviewees remember being naturally curious about people at a young age, which made it very easy for them to connect to and relate with others.

But most (if not all) Super Connectors I've met have honed their craft over years of practice, and have learned various skills and traits, such as how to build trust, how to increase emotional intelligence, how to curate and run communities, and so on, that make them so effective.

It's like being an athlete. You might be born with natural abilities to become a world-class athlete, but without years of training and practice, you're not likely to realize your full potential. In a similar way, many Super Connectors were born with the traits that enable them to become great but have had to learn the traits and skills over the years to become great at it.

Maybe more to the point, most people can become better athletes if they choose to learn and practice. Similarly, more people can become better connectors simply by learning the traits and skills described in this book.

4. **How large of a "scale" are we talking about?**

I haven't seen a hard limit to the number of people that Super Connectors know, but my interviewees have networks of thousands to tens of thousands of people (and, in a few cases, hundreds of thousands of people).

It's important to distinguish between knowing people versus. being in active dialog with them. Super Connectors are also limited by time, energy, and bandwidth and cannot actively engage bi-directionally with more than, say, a few hundred people in a given time period. But they can keep their relationships warm and active with far more people over longer periods of time, and then reconnect with them easily with a high level of familiarity and trust.

The more relevant question is, "Why?" Why know tens of thousands of people? Why go through all that effort?

For Super Connectors, their "why" for having large networks is not to have a large network. In fact, the ones I've met do not really talk about the size of their networks. It's not something that defines them.

Instead, Super Connectors have large networks as a result of their pursuit of a higher purpose or goal. As you'll see in the following chapters, each of the Super Connector archetypes does specific things to help other people, and in doing so, they end up making lots of meaningful connections that expand into large networks of people.

5. Why Archetypes?

The Oxford English dictionary defines an "archetype" as "a very typical example of a certain person or thing." I've found it easiest to describe who the various Super Connectors are by grouping their related activities into the archetypes they embody.

Let's go back to the analogy of an athlete to explain. A basketball player is very different from a soccer player, but they are both archetypes of different kinds of athletes. If you want to become a better athlete, there are some core traits you must develop for any sport (such as cardiovascular strength, flexibility, and so forth), but you also have to hone the skills needed for a specific sport (such as dribbling with your hands versus dribbling with your feet).

Just as not all athletes are the same, not all Super Connectors are the same. There are distinct archetypes with their own individual specialties, and it's helpful to understand each one.

6. Are all Super Connectors "good" people?

Based on the definition and description of Super Connectors in this chapter, one might think that I'm saying that Super Connectors are all somehow "good" or "better" than others, morally and ethically superior. I'm not, and it's more nuanced than that.

First, Super Connectors are obviously all human, just like you and me, and as such, have their character flaws, their good and bad days, their baggage to carry, their "shadow selves" to work on, and so forth.

But if we define Super Connectors as "people who are exceptional at building, maintaining, and deepening trusted, meaningful relationships across social boundaries and at scale," then to be successful, they have to be trust builders, emotionally intelligent, generous with their time, capable of seeing past social differences and connecting with others as fellow brothers and sisters. To the extent we consider these traits "good," we can deem such a person to be that way also.

But let's ask this question: Are all doctors "good," meaning morally and ethically superior to others? Of course not. What they are able to *do* is good for humanity (healing people), and to be successful they must be educated, trained, and have the skills to be effective, including good bedside manners. The same is true for Super Connectors.

What matters most here is *choice*. Does the Super Connector use her power to help other people or to advance only herself? Does the Super Connector help one group of people oppress another or enable the various communities to come together and help one another?

For people with this gift, they have a clear choice to make, and as flawed as they may be as human beings, they can choose to use their Super Connector skills and power for enormous good in the world.

ACKNOWLEDGMENTS

I would like to thank the following people who have in their own way helped me on this journey:

My parents, without whose courage, sacrifice and hard work our lives would not have been possible. My sister, whose unending support and sass have helped me to stay motivated and grounded.

All of the Super Connectors and brilliant people I've had the privilege to meet and speak with during my research. Thank you for sharing your wisdom with me, and for doing your work to connect people and bring the world together.

In particular, I'd like to thank the following, whose stories grace the pages of this book and help illustrate the various archetypes. In order of appearance, Anna Morgenstern, Tony Leng, Nora Paxton, Nick Garbis, Mike MacCombie, Vanessa DiMauro, Ryan Groves, Shannon Lucas, Eric Larsen, Rob Cross, Bob Stone, Manoj Govindan, Arabella DeLucco, Lorine Pendleton, Arno Michaelis, Sir Robert Swan, Beth Dochinger, Shiva Sapkota, Carlito Rofoli, Barry Palte, Elizabeth Patterson, David Homan and Adria Dunn.

Others I'd like to thank include the following:

Ralph Loura, Michael Keithley, Diana McKenzie, Angela Yochem, Chris Yeh, and Summer Watson for your early and ongoing support.

Peter Sims, for urging me to "Slay the dragon, one scale at a time."

Shannon Lucas, for connecting me to Georges Sassine, and Georges for becoming my writing buddy and lifelong friend.

Tucker Max and others at Scribe Media for sharing your wisdom and providing the structure I needed to get the "vomit draft" completed.

Andra Pool and the amazing team at the Greenhouse (dba Greenhouse Scholars). Please keep doing what you're doing.

Fran Kirmser for "Blessed Unrest" and more.

All of my friends in the West Coast Swing dance community who have given me so much joy on the dance floor, along with your friendship and support. In particular, Valerie, Lisa, Jenna, Jason, Yenni and Warren, Erin, Susan, Kelly Casanova, and the crew in Maui (808), among others.

All my fellow collaborators and "co-conspirators" in the various communities including Samudra, BLKSHP, the Vine, the Research Board, and the Collaboratory, among others.

Charles Vogl for insisting on doing the right thing.

Gabriel Grant, Harry Pickens, and the other beautiful souls at the Byron Fellowship whose love and support gave me the energy I needed to finish my manuscript.

All of my other friends near and far, including Simon Mulcahy, Shubber Ali, Phillip Kiracofe, Dave Zaboski, Brian Kennedy, Elay Cohen, Abby Kramer, John Williams, Megan Dahlgren and others who have been steadfast in their support.

"M" for presenting me with the opportunity to use the negative as fuel for the positive. Cindy, Lydia, and Sparrow for your inspirations along the way.

My publisher, Tyler Wagner, for helping me to finish this project, and my editor, Sherman Morrison, for your timely and thoughtful edits.

To our Creator, God, Yahweh, Allah, Source, Universe or whatever other name we use for the universal consciousness and source of unconditional love from which we all spring, and to which we will all return.

To all the other Connectors (Super or otherwise) whom I haven't met yet. Thank you for what you do to help make the world better.

To you, the reader: Thank you for helping me to complete this journey.